Mario Reading was born in Dorset, and brought up in England, Germany, and the South of France. He studied Comparative Literature at the University of East Anglia, where he specialized in French and German literature and translation. He spoke four languages. During a nomadic youth he sold rare books, taught riding in Africa, studied dressage in Vienna, played polo in India, Spain and Dubai, ran a seventy-horse polo stables in Gloucestershire, and helped manage his Mexican wife's coffee plantation.

In recent years he established a worldwide reputation as an original and groundbreaking expert on Nostradamus. He is the author of the original bestselling edition of this book, *Nostradamus: The Complete Prophecies for the Future* and also of *Nostradamus: The Good News* and *Nostradamus & The Third Antichrist*, as well as the ultimate collection of Nostradamus's prophecies: *The Complete Nostradamus*. His Nostradamus Trilogy, comprising *The Nostradamus Prophecies*, *The Mayan Codex* and *The Third Antichrist* – thrillers based on the theme of Nostradamus's 58 missing prophecies – has become an international bestseller, with rights to date sold in 38 countries. Mario appeared in a number of documentaries on Nostradamus for, amongst others, the Discovery Channel, the National Geographic Channel, and the History Channel. He was also voted into the Top 100 Spiritually Influential Living People by *Mind, Body, Spirit* magazine.

He passed away on 29 January 2017.

NOSTRADAMUS

THE COMPLETE PROPHECIES
FOR THE FUTURE

MARIO READING

WATKINS

Sharing Wisdom Since 1893

This edition first published in the UK and USA in 2015 by
Watkins, an imprint of Watkins Media Limited
Unit 11, Shepperton House
89 Shepperton Road
London N1 3DF

enquiries@watkinspublishing.com

13 15 17 19 20 18 16 14 12

Designed and Typeset by Clare Thorpe

Printed and bound in the United Kingdom by TJ Books Ltd

A CIP record for this book is available from the British Library

ISBN: 978-1-78028-897-0

www.watkinspublishing.com

MIX
Paper from
responsible sources
FSC® C013056
FSC
www.fsc.org

CONTENTS

A Note on the Author xii

Introduction to the 2015 Edition.. 1

Preamble 7

Biographical Note 9

The Prophecies

2001: Twin Towers Disaster I 18

          Twin Towers Disaster II 20

2002: Guantanamo Bay 22

2003: US/Iraq War I 24

          US/Iraq War II 26

          US/Iraq War III 28

          US/Iraq War IV 30

          Aung San Suu Kyi & Burma's Military Junta 32

2004: Tsunami I 35

2005: Death of Pope John Paul II 37

          New Orleans Floods 40

2006: Crisis in the Protestant Church 42

          Pope Benedict XVI 45

          Assassination of a World Leader 48

          Aftermath of Pope John Paul II's Death 52

2007: North Korean Crisis 55

2008: Financial Meltdown/Credit Crunch 58

          Religious Revival 60

2010: Advance Warning of Third Antichrist 63

2011: Global Warming I 65

   Dangers to John Paul II's Successor, Benedict XVI 67

2012: Death of a Pope I 69

   Princess Diana & Dodi Fayed 71

2013: Nuclear Fission 74

   Abortion Debate Reignites in the Catholic
   Church 76

2014: Death of a Pope II 79

2015: Famine Relief 81

   Hillary Clinton 83

2016: Ecological Disasters I 85

   Ecological Disasters II 87

2017: Ecological Disasters III 90

   Scandals in the Roman Catholic Church I 92

   Scandals in the Roman Catholic Church II 94

   Scandals in the Roman Catholic Church III 96

2018: Islamic Attack on a Northern French Port 98

2019: Emmanuel Macron 100

   UK Fails to Exit the European Union 102

2021: Terrorist Attack in Southern France 104

   Birth of an Island 106

2022: Succession to the UK Throne 108

   Abdication of Charles III of England 110

   Poor Sir Bevis 112

2023: New First Family – Precursor 115

2024: New First Family 117

2025: Sunni/Shiite War 119

2027: Six Lucky Gamblers 122

2028: Discovery of the Philosopher's Stone 125

2029: The Sun I 127

The Sun II 129

2030 The Sun is Blotted Out & Secrets Lost 132

2032: Political Correctness I 134

Birth of the Third Antichrist – Presage I 136

Birth of the Third Antichrist – Presage II 138

US Presidential Election 140

2033: Class War 142

2034: Political Correctness II 144

Political Correctness III 146

Birth of the Third Antichrist – Presage III 148

2035: Winter Freeze 150

Birth of the Third Antichrist 152

2036: Birth of the Third Antichrist – Consequences 155

2037: War Between Australia & Indonesia 157

2039: Greco-Turkish Problem 159

2040: Great Storm 161

End of Monarchy in Britain I 163

End of Monarchy in Britain II 165

End of Monarchy in Britain III 167

2041: Birth of a Visionary Pan-African Leader 169

2043: Religious Wars I 171

Religious Wars II 173

2044: Chemical Warfare 175

2045: Catholic/Jewish Miscegenation 178

2046: Collective Unconscious 181

Meteor Strikes as Harbingers of Change 183

2047: Mafia Killing I 185

Mafia Killing II 187

2048: Global Warming II 189

	US Hurricanes/Global Warming III	191
2049:	French Immigration	193
2051:	Terrorism	195
2052:	Emancipation of Muslim Women	197
2053:	Battle of the Sexes	199
	Book Burning	201
2054:	Monsoon Rains	204
	US/Chinese Standoff	206
2055:	US/Chinese False Dawn	208
	Islam Disturbs the Balance of World Power I	210
	Islam Disturbs the Balance of World Power II	212
2056:	Islam Disturbs the Balance of World Power III	214
	Crisis in the Roman Catholic Church I	216
	Crisis in the Roman Catholic Church II	218
	Crisis in the Roman Catholic Church III	220
2057:	Crisis in the Roman Catholic Church IV	222
	Crisis in the Roman Catholic Church V	224
2059:	Buddhism & the Protestant Church	226
2060:	England Secedes from European Union	228
	Serbo-Croatian Conflict	230
2061:	French Leadership	232
	Arab War	234
2062:	Worldwide Epidemic	236
2063:	Peace Reigns over the Earth	239
2064:	Consequences of England's Secession from EU	241
2065:	Treaty of Rome	243
	Dangers of Embryo Replacement	245
2066:	England & Scotland Fall Out over EU	248
2067:	Great Famine	250
2068:	Nuclear Market in New Europe	252

2069: Warnings of Global War 254

An Asteroid Strikes the Earth 256

2070: Global War I 258

Global War II 260

Global War III 263

Global War IV 265

2071: Global War V 267

2075: Global War Aftermath/End of Phoenix Period 269

Third Antichrist I 271

2077: Third Antichrist II 274

Fortress Britain Following Global War 276

2078: Civil Disobedience Begins 278

2079: Change of World Order 280

2080: Climate Change Due to Global War 282

Tsunami II 284

2081: Tsunami III 286

New Leader Appears 289

2082: European Earthquake 291

Locust Plague 293

2083: US Earthquake 295

2084: Aftermath of the Coming of the

Third Antichrist 397

The Final Pope 399

2085: French Crisis Prelude I 301

The Future of Israel 303

2089: Cyprus Partition 305

US & China See Eye to Eye 307

2090: Hungary in Crisis 309

Greek Nuclear Accident 311

2091: Twenty Years Since End of Global War 313

2095: French Crisis Prelude II 315

Ecological Burn-Out 317

2096: Secularization of a Superstate 319

The Emergence of a New Religious Sect 321

2097: The Middle East 323

2098: French Crisis I 325

2099: French Crisis II 327

2100: French Crisis III 329

Franco-British Crisis 331

2101: French Crisis IV 333

2103: Global Warming IV/Mediterranean Famine 335

2105: Submarine Warfare 337

7048: Nostradamus Takes His Leave 339

7073: The Great Comedian 342

7074: Armageddon/The Final Prophecy 344

Index 348

Power will be given

to overcautious fools...

NOSTRADAMUS

QUATRAIN NUMBER

2 / 9 5

A NOTE ON THE AUTHOR

Mario Reading died on 29 January 2017, and is sorely missed by family and friends. He was only 63 and had been suffering from cancer for half his life. His obituary in the *Daily Telegraph* recorded that, 'despite his ill health Reading, a burly, attractive man who talked frankly about his illnesses but never indulged in self-pity, gave the impression to those who met him of being as strong as an ox.'

The Times, describing Mario as a 'linguist and adventurer renowned for his occasionally broad interpretations of the prophecies of the French seer Nostradamus', pointed out with similar appreciation that 'Reading – a considerable scholar, who also wrote thrillers and was an authority on Mayan and Catholic mysticism – devoted much of his life to getting it right.'

These are fine tributes to a fine man. Mario and I sometimes collaborated on writing work, and I have been happy to help with this further edition of the *Prophecies for the Future*. There are some changes to the interpretations of a small number of predictions as they appeared in the previous edition of the book, based on Mario's notes and a conversation we had not long before he died.

Ned Halley, 2017

INTRODUCTION TO THE 2015 EDITION

༄

When I originally wrote this book in 2005 (for a 2006 publication date) I made much of my assumption that quatrain 10/26 – 2006–2008: Assassination of a World Leader, might well serve as a warning to President Bush's bodyguards to be especially careful of their President's welfare during the three-year period covered by the quatrain. In the event, although there were a number of plots against the US President during that period, I am very happy to say that none of them were successful. Mrs Benazir Bhutto, however, surely a 'world leader' of the first magnitude, and very probably the next President of Pakistan, was assassinated exactly within my time frame, on 27 December 2007 (her assassination occurred exactly two weeks before the 2008 Pakistani elections). I am not proud of interpreting Nostradamus's prophecy correctly – neither, presumably, would Nostradamus have been. He saw political murder as an unnecessary evil, and his instinct would have been that forewarned is very probably forearmed, and that all world leaders in the public eye would have done well, during that particularly fraught period in international politics, to have taken especial care of themselves.

Four further prophecies that I made in 2005 may now, with the benefit of hindsight, be seen to have hit the spot. They are 3/6 – 2006: Crisis in the Protestant Church; 3/7 – 2007: North Korean Crisis; 4/11 – 2011: Dangers to John Paul II's Successor, Benedict XVI; and 1/18: Islamic Attack on a Northern French Port. All are fully explained in my author's notes, which follow the original prophecies. Apart from that I have made only two important changes to the original manuscript – I have moved quatrains 8/28 and 2/28 from 2028 to 2008 for reasons which, when my author's notes are read, will soon become obvious. The 2008 Credit Crunch has been a world-shattering event, and it is quite clear that Nostradamus called and dated it correctly – it was I who made the assumption that the events would occur in 2028, not him – in fact his quatrain numbers are quite uncannily prescient. So Nostradamus triumphs again – go read the quatrains and see why.

Now back to the *Complete Prophecies for the Future*. I have begun the commentaries marginally in the past, with the Twin Towers Disaster of 11 September 2001, not only because it coincided almost exactly with the turn of our century, but also because Nostradamus's predictions about the event are so detailed, and so astonishing, that they will give even further credence to his prognostications for both our future, and that of our planet. Interpreting Nostradamus is very much like working on a detective story. Following his filigrees of meaning through to a final, if tentative, conclusion, is an immensely satisfying work of deduction. I have therefore taken as my starting point the premise that the most esoteric of Nostradamus's quatrains – in other words those without any obvious reference to the times in which he lived, or to the four and a half centuries immediately succeeding his death – must, by default, refer to the future. I have therefore retranslated these, and approached them entirely afresh, without referring back to past commentaries.

Old French spellings are eccentric, to say the least, and both proper names and nouns can be spelled in a variety of ways. Meanings themselves were considered far more fluid then than they would be now, and an absolutely literal interpretation of any text would have been scoffed at by educated sixteenth-century readers. What is entirely new about my approach concerns the interrelation between quatrains – one feeds from the other, as it were. By adhering to Nostradamus's own index dates when dealing with prophecies relating to the future, connections were found across *The Centuries* which threw an extraordinary collective light onto the meanings of individual, often opaque, prophecies.

Commentators in the past have approached all the quatrains individually, as separate predictions, but Nostradamus was an alchemist and a scryer, and he believed in mixing things, and from that admixture, truth would come. Alchemists believed that everything on earth was fused and inter-relatable and that one only had to discover the secret of this to reach hidden codes and morphological secrets. Many of the quatrains, although nominally stemming from different Nostradamian *Centuries*, are, in fact, closely interconnected and interrelated, and can only be correctly construed when this is borne in mind. This fact, this interrelation, only comes to light when one is in the actual process of interpreting them – one quatrain feeds off the other, and a true interpretation can only be reached when this is taken into account. Previous commentators have simply not listened enough to Nostradamus's index dating.

There is even an argument, to which I give some credence, that Nostradamus may have intended the quatrains as a sort of rolling commentary on history – that he meant them to be used over and over again, in other words, and that they were only fully interpretable after the event.

Nostradamus organized his quatrains into *Centuries* of one hundred quatrains apiece (save for the seventh in the series of ten, which stops at number forty-two). It is probable that he originally intended the quatrain numbers to correspond directly to years in the calendar, but then chickened out for fear of the Inquisition. However the skeleton of his original structure still remains. Very often quatrains that may seem rather insipid if taken alone, gain in interest and clarity when taken in the context of other quatrains, appearing in different *Centuries*, but with similar index years. This is particularly true of quatrains that foretell (in Nostradamian terms, of course) the distant future. By the use of these parallels, a picture can be summoned up of a time far in the future, and of the events which invest it.

Many of the index dates link together categorically, in terms of meaning, with similar index dates in different Centuries, for even though many years may separate the time of writing, they still apply to the very same events. A good example would be the global war scenario in quatrains 10/69, 5/70, 9/70, 2/70, 8/70, and 3/71, which predict events in the years 2069–2071. Another would be the French Crisis sequence of 10/98, 6/99, 1/100, 2/100, and 10/1, which cover the years 2098–2101. Or how about the Crisis in the Roman Catholic Church series, in quatrains 2/56, 5/56, 4/56, 10/57 and 2/57, with a year span of 2056–2057? Or the End of Monarchy in Britain cycle, of 10/40, 4/40 and 5/40, year span 2040? Look at the index dates – they are absolutely specific.

As are the connections between the quatrains. And no one has noticed this before!

Far too little account has been taken, in the past, of classical references and mythologies in Nostradamus's writings. These would have formed the fundamental basis of Nostradamus's thinking processes – even the concept of the Oracle, which Nostradamus personified, was taken from that of Delphi. Nostradamus would, like any educated man in sixteenth-century France, have had a vast body of classical learning at his fingertips, and would have considered its use, and his readers' understanding of classical myth, as a *sine qua non*. A similar wellhead of knowledge needs to be used when interpreting the quatrains today, and negates any half-baked ideas that Nostradamus wrote in a secret code, or Green Language, accessible only to privileged initiates, or to those versed in the secret lore of the Akashic Chronicle. He was, quite simply, extremely well read and well educated.

The French are traditionally fond of word play, and in Nostradamus's time no one would have dreamt of assuming that a word meant simply what it was purported to mean within the context of a single sentence – the larger context, too, would need to be taken into account. I'll give you an example. An apparently straightforward Old French phrase such as '*En Normandie l'on vendange avec la gaule*', which, taken literally would appear to mean, 'In Normandy they harvest with a pole', can also mean, 'In Normandy, they even harvest beside Frenchmen', or, alternatively, 'The Poles are the vintagers in Normandy'. Irritating for translators, yes, but also enormously rich in potential seams of gold and hidden meanings.

The key to Nostradamus, in my opinion, is in the actual process of translation – the act of translating opens the commentator's mind to what Nostradamus, through the centuries (both literally and metaphorically) is trying to tell him. The most important thing for a translator is never to translate line by line. The whole quatrain must always be considered, and one is often forced to return to the beginning when the final meaning becomes clear. Wishful thinking is the translator's greatest danger – the temptation to plump on one possible answer because it appears obvious. Because we commentators are not, by default, Nostradamus himself, we are condemned to approach him retrospectively. This, needless to say, sets us up for accusations of closing the stable door after the horse has bolted. By addressing only the future, I am secretly rather hoping to avoid that criticism, but I acknowledge that any commentary on Nostradamus that invokes such a future is invested by the commentator's own, inevitably limited, knowledge of the present, and the limits of the commentator's own innate imaginative capacities.

The only answer to this dilemma is for the commentator to approach the quatrains with an open mind, and the capacity to be surprised in a serendipitous manner. I trust that, when you read the commentaries which follow, you will feel that I have done this.

PREAMBLE

The idea that any historian or biographer is 'right', or is creating more than yet another believable and interesting myth to overlay and influence an already existing myth, is fundamentally absurd. Few people can even describe the day that has just passed accurately – let alone decades, if not centuries, before their own time. No, what historians and biographers are giving us is an informed opinion, and a vastly subjective one at that, dependent on the often sparse material that has been left, frequently as a result of random historical happenstance, and to which they inevitably ascribe – because they have a vested interest in so doing – far too much significance.

The winners in history customarily hide what is inconvenient to them, or manipulate the truth to suit the scale of their ambitions, and the losers bleat, or are written out of history altogether (Mithraism being but one obvious example) – that is, after all, human nature. When losers do out-survive those they feel have done them (or their cabal) wrong, as often as not they try to rewrite history the better to reinforce their feelings of outrage and despair – that too is human nature. All history is therefore fiction disguised as fact, but actually representing the historians' best shot at an almost-truth. It is for exactly this reason that apocryphal stories, hearsay, and scandal are potentially just as historically relevant as (purported) dry facts, government documents (a likely story), and contemporary commentaries (untarnished, of course, by even the merest hint of vainglory!).

Wars have been fought over lesser issues than the details of Nostradamus's alleged biography. Scholars have been declaring that only they know the true story from as far back as the late sixteenth century, and their descendants still continue to do so today (and with equal impunity). So little is actually known about Nostradamus's life, however, that some of the more apocryphal stories, often emerging a century or so after his death, become important pointers in themselves – not so much to the 'real life' (as if anyone is capable of teasing that out from the mass of obfuscation, forgery, and hearsay that underlies much Nostradamus scholarship) as to the life he ought to have led, given the reality of his influence.

Anyway, here is a short biographical note that does not purport to be the exact truth (what can?) so much as to coalesce both given, disputed, and established facts into some sort of sensible (if inevitably fallible) order.

BIOGRAPHICAL NOTE

The medieval France *profonde* in which Michel de Nostredame (1503–66) grew up encompassed a mass of different sects, tribes, and communities, but with no truly effective central government. Villagers from the Pyrenees or from deepest Provence, for instance, might never have heard of Paris, nor would they have understood Parisian French if it were spoken to them – faces, manners, and even language varied alarmingly according to the contours of the valleys in which people lived. Isolated communities were surrounded by a ripple-effect of further enclaves, mini-fiefdoms, clan centres (often with bells delineating tribal territories), and racial diversifications, dating all the way back to pre-history – a charivari that remained in place well into the nineteenth century, with distant echoes of its dying fall still reverberating today.

Few French people had ever seen a map of France. Fewer still were aware of French history as a definable, ongoing process. Of the total population, ninety-eight per cent were deemed to be Catholic, it is true, but with marked variations in religious practice. Local priests competed with quacks, witches, healers, simple-mongers, and weather merchants for the hearts and souls of their parish. Before the French Revolution (1789–99), the word 'France' was merely used to describe a truncated area in and around Paris. In Provence, someone from the north might be termed a *Franciot* or *Franchiman*, and the Provençal-born and Francoprovençal-speaking Nostradamus would most probably have grown up with a quasi-atavistic mistrust of both the royal government and its motivations (largely on account of a cultural and linguistic bifurcation that was only really addressed by the Abbé Henri Grégoire at the time of the 1793–94 Reign of Terror).

For Nostradamus, it must be remembered, was both a committed, mainline Catholic, and an ethnic – and therefore potentially ostracisable – Jew. If that sounds like a paradox, it wasn't perceived as such in a sixteenth-century France dedicated to both God, in the form of the Inquisition, and mammon, in the form of the pillaging of others' property for reasons of ecclesiastical expediency. For thirty years, under the reign of Good King René, the Jews of Provence had been accorded the free practice of their religion, but all that ended with René's death in 1480, a date which unfortunately coincided with the inception of the Spanish Inquisition.

By the time of Nostradamus's birth, in 1503, most prominent Jews had prudently converted to a pragmatic form of Catholicism, thanks to the edicts of, respectively, Charles VIII in 1488, and Louis XII in 1501. This didn't prevent the French Crown from occasionally plundering their possessions, but it did offer them a measure of protection in a country suddenly rife with religious intolerance and paranoia. So the infant Michel de Nostredame found himself both uncircumcised (the penalty for which, under Levitical law, is ostracism from the congregation of Israel), and baptized according to the Christian rite, whilst retaining, in the form of his maternal great-grandfather, Jean de Saint-Rémy, an intimate access to the Jewish chain of tradition, the Schalscheleth Ha-Kabbalah, which was to stand him in very good stead in his later incarnation as a diviner and scryer.

As a result of this upbringing, Nostradamus almost

certainly dabbled in magic, and very certainly in mysticism and the kabbalah, which encapsulated the Jewish search for new wisdom in a creative synthesis between the mythologies of ancient Egypt, ancient Greece, Assyrian astrology, Babylonian magic, Arabian divination, Platonic philosophy, and Gnosticism (Gershom Scholem, in his *Major Trends in Jewish Mysticism* writes that 'it can be taken as certain that ... ancient writings, with Gnostic excerpts written in Hebrew, made their way from the East to Provence ... to become one of the chief influences which shaped the theosophy of the thirteenth-century kabbalists').

The secretive and mystical nature of the kabbalah, therefore, would have provided a much-needed escape from the grim realities of Jewish life in an Inquisitorial Europe, and a much-needed panacea in the face of the forcible conversions that followed René's death. By pure chance, Nostradamus's native town of St-Rémy was the perfect place to study the kabbalah, as Provence was generally acknowledged as home to the earliest kabbalistic community in France. Paradoxically, perhaps, Nostradamus, as well as being a kabbalist, an alchemist, and a Talmudist, was also a fervent adherent to Catholic doctrine throughout his life, and would certainly not have been accepted at Avignon University (not then a part of France) had he not been sincere in these assertions, and in his excoriation of the near ubiquitous Lutheran heresy. He later enrolled, again without problem, at the venerable University of Montpellier (founded in 1220) in order to study medicine – a wise move, as Montpellier possessed, without doubt, the greatest school of medicine of those times.

After matriculating from Montpellier (from which he had briefly been expelled on 3 October 1529, for the alleged crime of having practised as an apothecary, before being readmitted, third time lucky, on 23 October that same year) – and following hard upon an invigilation process that would have been conducted in the medieval manner of a formal dispute between the student and the teaching staff, rather than merely by written examination – Nostradamus was plunged straight into the treatment of an outbreak of the plague

Encumbered by the usual paraphernalia worn by medical practitioners during such crises (Irish physician Neil O'Glacan (1590–1655), in his *Tractatus de Peste* (Toulouse 1629), describes plague doctors as wearing long leather gowns stained with many different coloured powders, gauntlets, leather masks with glass protection for the eyes, and a long sponge-filled beak imbued with fumigants for the nose), Nostradamus struck out into entirely new territory with his invention of a purifying powder (his 'rose pill'), which, we are led to believe, inspired an entirely untypical confidence in his patients. As a direct consequence of this experience, Nostradamus became something of an authority on the plague, a talent that was sorely tested when plague struck, once again, during his tenure as a doctor at Agen, killing his young wife and their two children. As a result, Nostradamus not only suffered from the usual criticism of 'Physician, heal thyself', but was also sued by the distraught family of his wife for the return of her dowry.

Traumatized by his loss, Nostradamus took to the road, and travelled through many parts of France, Italy, and Sicily, before finally settling in Salon de Provence. There, at the age of forty-four, he met a widow, Anne Ponsarde Gemelle (*gemellus* implies a twin in Latin), whom he married on 11 November 1547. They moved into a house on the Rue Ferreiraux (now known as Rue Nostradamus), and Nostradamus, in considerable demand by this time, not least for his sovereign remedies, continued his travels.

It was during this period that, thanks to his meetings with apothecaries, physicians and magicians, he first began to suspect that he had the gift of prophecy and second sight. He was not the only one. Under the reign of the thirteen Valois kings, it was estimated that there were upwards of 30,000 astrologers, sorcerers, alchemists, and prophets practising in Paris alone, and it is to Nostradamus's credit, and to that of his art, that he rose, inexorably, to the top of a very crowded tree.

Three years after the publication of his *Traité des Fardemens* in 1552 (an *à la mode* treatise on unguents, jams and preserves of all kinds), Nostradamus followed up – rather tentatively, it must be said – with the first edition of his famous *Centuries* (1555), fearing, according to his pupil Jean Aymes de Chavigny, both castigation and mockery. The 353 quatrains, to just about everybody's surprise, including that of Nostradamus, were a sensation. Summoned to Paris by Henri II's queen, Catherine de Medici, barely a year after its publication, Nostradamus returned to Salon a rich man, having discovered, the hard way, that private practice (the casting of personal horoscopes and the alleviation of courtiers' ailments) was considerably more remunerative, and a good deal less precarious, than celebrity stargazing. Nostradamus continued to advise the queen, however, not least because she protected him, in some measure, from falling foul of the religious authorities for blasphemy, while her regal favour afforded him a much-appreciated kudos and the promise of a steady income.

In terms of the apparent dangers Nostradamus faced from the Inquisition, it is important to draw a distinction, just as Alexander of Hales (1183–1245) did, between the two principal, although different, forms of magic. Namely *divination* (from the Latin *divinitas*, meaning the godhead, or the divine nature), which was seen as High Magic; and *maleficum* or evil-doing (from the Latin *maleficus*, meaning hurtful or mischievous), which, in the Middle Ages, was the word coined to represent Low Magic. Low Magic was designed for instant gratification – the equivalent, in magical terms, of a caffeine hit. It might span the ritual burning of hair, the spearing of wax dolls, or sacrificial offerings leading to fruitful crops or the emergence of rain after a long dry spell. High Magic incorporated astrology and alchemy, and was built on a firm philosophical foundation, deriving as much from Pythagoras as it did from the Persian Magi, Gnosticism, or Neo-Platonism. Both were thus categorically different in origin, with Low Magic drawing much of its motive power from Aristotelianism. High Magic was therefore a subject of justifiable study, and if not quite 'nice', at least intellectually acceptable. Low Magic was considered akin to witchcraft.

Nostradamus, needless to say, was a High Magic figure, taking his cue from the *Corpus Hermeticum*, a magical treatise believed, in medieval times, to be of the highest antiquity, but later proved by Isaac Casaubon (no relation, beyond the obvious, to George Eliot's fictional *Middlemarch* antihero) to have been composed circa the second or third century AD – Casaubon's opinion carried great weight, as, in his day (1559–1614) he was considered, alongside the Agen-born Joseph Scaliger, to be the most learned man in Europe.

Nostradamus's adherence to High Magic, therefore, provided him with considerable protection from Inquisitorial probing, and, alongside his support from the queen, made it even more likely that he did not have either the need or the motivation to hide or codify his index dates. This High Magic itinerary of Nostradamus's also tallies with his pedagogical intentions – for he truly believed that mankind was subject to an overweening fate, and that nothing in history occurred as the result of accident. Everything was either intended or preprogrammed, and as such could be teased out through scrying, divination, necromancy, hydromancy, chiromancy, astrology, dream interpretation, the study of ancient texts, numerology, alchemy, the kabbalah, hermetic inference, and the manipulation of the fundamental chemical composition of inanimate objects. With each step in the divinatory cycle, the adept was led to a higher level of understanding, which culminated in a process of mental and spiritual purification leading to absolute clarity of thought. Such a spiritual catharsis allowed the adept access to hidden truths that, with the best possible of intentions, he would then lay before the world to make of them what it willed.

Such apparent self-glorification was frowned on by the religious community, but it wasn't, for the most part, considered witchcraft, and its zealots were allowed to practise, to all intents and purposes, unmolested. However, magic was, most definitely, anti-clerical, in the sense that many of its adherents believed that they had been specifically chosen to express God's intentions, rather than simply to respond to them, as a priest or a true believer would. To this extent alone was Nostradamus in danger, and he reacted to such allegations by making it clear, on numerous occasions, that he did not feel himself to be a consciously chosen vessel, but merely a random one, selected by happenstance.

Consciously chosen vessel or not, the summit of Nostradamus's stratospherical celebrity career came during a royal visit to Salon itself, in 1564, by the boy king, Charles IX (who would later, at his dominant mother's instigation, approve the St Bartholomew's Day Massacre). Catherine invited Nostradamus and his family to a private visit at the royal apartments, and then to a further consultation, where she asked him to cast the horoscope of her youngest son, the Duke of Anjou. Nostradamus was more interested in the young Henri de Navarre, however, and even investigated the ten-year-old child whilst he was sleeping, predicting that he would eventually inherit all of France.

Thanks to the evidence contained in Nostradamus's last will and testament, we know that he must have been very well paid for his troubles, a factor that must have provided him with considerable comfort during his two declining years, for, assailed by gout, arthritis, and a heart condition that even his own sovereign remedies failed to alleviate, he finally succumbed on 2 July 1566, in exactly the fashion he had predicted for himself.

THE
PROPHECIES

TWIN TOWERS DISASTER I

SEPTEMBER 2001

1 / 8 7

Ennosigée, feu du centre de terre,

Fera trembler au tour de Cité Neufve;

Deux grands rochers long temps feront la guerre,

Puis Arethusa rougira nouveau Fleuve.

ϪϠ

Earthshaking, a fire from the centre of the earth

Will shake the towers of the New City

As a result, two great rocks will fight a long war

Until Arethusan springs bloody the river afresh.

An uncanny foretelling of the Twin Towers disaster, even down to a paralleling of the two rock-like towers with a war between the 'two great rocks' of Christianity and Islam. The towers are brought down by fire drawn from the earth's core, an extraordinary leap of the imagination for Nostradamus when one bears in mind that the explosive catalyst used in the attacks was oil-based aviation fuel. Another extraordinary coincidence links the myth of Arethusa, with her legendary springs at Ellis, to that of Ellis Island, the immigration gateway to New York – a buried clue left by Nostradamus which pinpoints exactly to which New City he is referring in his text.

A further clue to the location of the disaster is contained in the first line's use of the word *du*, which can mean either 'of' or 'from'. If read as 'fire *of* the centre of the earth', then the World Trade Centre tellingly springs to mind. Nostradamus's use of the term *Cité Neufve* (the New City), immediately links 1/87 to the next quatrain in our series, 10/49 – 2001. Other similarities also grab the attention; the mention of rocks and mountains; the symbols of water and its poisoning, the first time with blood, the second with sulphur; and the Arethusan springs, at both Ellis and Syracuse (also a place in New York State).

SUMMARY

Following an attack on New York's Twin Towers, in which aviation fuel is the principle component, a long war between Christianity and Islam is triggered.

TWIN TOWERS DISASTER II

SEPTEMBER 2001

10/49

Jardin du monde au pres du cité neufve,

Dans le chemin des montaignes cavees,

Sera saisi et plongé dans la Cuve,

Beuvant par force eaux soulfre envenimees.

The world's garden near the New City

In the roadway, hollow mountains,

They will be seized, and plunged into
the sewers

People will be forced to drink the
sulphur-poisoned waters.

A chilling image of the Twin Towers, which Nostradamus describes, in the only way he is able, given the limitations of the period in which he is living, as 'hollow mountains in the roadway'. We already know, from 1/87 – 2001, that his 'New City' is New York. Here he presents a terrifying picture of the two skyscrapers being 'plunged into the sewers', descriptions that could have been taken direct from television news pictures of the disaster showing the towers crumpling inexorably earthwards. 'Sulphur-poisoned waters' can be taken both figuratively and as a metaphor for the realization, by the United States, that from this moment on, they, too, are vulnerable, and that they will be forced to drain the cup of poisoned water fate has handed them to its dregs.

SUMMARY

The destruction of the Twin Towers will traumatize the people of the United States. There will be many long-term effects of the tragedy, and it will poison relations between the US and Islam.

GUANTANAMO BAY

Les exilez deportez dans les isles,
Au changement d'un plus cruel monarque
Seront meurtris: et mis deux les scintiles,
Qui de parler ne seront estez parques.

༽

The exiles are deported to the islands

When the new leader proves even crueller

There are murders; two at a time they will
be questioned

Until they cannot stop speaking.

More than five hundred political detainees were transferred from Camp X-Ray to the newly built Camp Delta at Guantanamo Bay (which forms part of the Cuban archipelago, ergo 'the islands') following the defeat of the Taliban in Afghanistan in 2002. After the US/Iraq war of 2003, even more 'exiles' were transferred there. In Ba'athist terms, President Bush would be perceived as an even 'crueller' leader than Saddam Hussein, and countless murders have been committed as a direct result of US intervention in both countries. The Bush regime, embarrassed by the bad publicity over its treatment of the internees, has since struggled to establish a legally viable argument to justify its harsh interrogation techniques at Guantanamo, which, as one US official dryly commented, is the 'legal equivalent of outer space'. It is reasonable to suppose that prisoners, on the receiving end of such techniques, would very often talk 'until they cannot stop speaking'.

SUMMARY

Survivors of the war in Afghanistan are deported to Guantanamo Bay. One prisoner's testimony is used against the other. The prisoners, under intolerable pressure, are eventually forced to talk.

US/IRAQ WAR I

MARCH/APRIL 2003

7/7

Sur le combat des grans cheveux, legiers
On criera le grand croissant confound
De nuict tuer monts, habits de bergiers
Abismes rouges dans le fossé profond.

ℰ

As a result of the war started by the mighty
light-haired ones

People will cry out that the great crescent of
Islam is confounded

At night, on the mountains, those dressed as
shepherds will die

Gulleys of blood will run through the
deep ditches.

An accurate foretelling of the war which occurred between the United States with its ally the United Kingdom (the mighty light-haired ones), and Iraq, during March and April 2003. Nostradamus implies that it will be wrongly assumed, following the conflict, that the might of Islam has been tamed. A terrible bloodbath will follow, with many Iraqis killed. Nostradamus's haunting image of blood running through the 'deep ditches' may suggest, as happened in Afghanistan during the war of October 2001, that a return to trench warfare will form part of the continuing conflict. If taken metaphorically, of course, the symbol of a 'ditch' accurately portrays the vast gulf remaining between both sides of the conflict, a gulf that will rapidly fill up with the dead and dying.

SUMMARY

The war against Islam will not be easily won by the Western powers. Many will die before an accommodation is reached. There will be times when the fighting reaches unprecedented levels of brutality.

US/IRAQ WAR II

MARCH/APRIL 2003

6/34

Du feu volant la machination
Viendra troubler au grand chef assiegez
Dedans sera telle sedition
Qu'en desespoir seront les profligez.

The contrivance of flying fire

Will come to trouble the besieged leader

Inside, there will be so much sedition

That the corrupt ones will despair.

This has a pretty clear connection with 6/97 - 2003 [US/ Iraq War III], with its use of the 'flying fire' and 'burning sky' analogies, together with the implication of a 'besieged' city, and its leader. By the end of his twenty-four-year hold on power, Saddam Hussein had become completely 'corrupt', and his autocracy knew, quite literally, no bounds. It is also perfectly possible to read line 1's 'contrivance of flying fire' as implying that Saddam would encounter problems with weapons of mass destruction, and that these would contribute to his downfall. We do know that he viciously put down all 'sedition' within the ranks of his Ba'athist party, even going so far as to have members of his own immediate family killed for disloyalty. All these factors, once taken together, make the quatrain particularly impressive.

SUMMARY

Saddam Hussein will be attacked from the sky. His own people will rise against him. He will belatedly recognize the mistakes he has made, but it will be too late to change the outcome of the attack.

US/IRAQ WAR III

MARCH/APRIL 2003

6/97

Cinq et quarante degrés ciel bruslera,

Feu approcher de la grand cité neufve,

Instant grand flamme esparse sautera,

Quand on voudra des Normans faire preuve.

ᘐ

The sky will burn those at 45 degrees

Fire will approach the great new city

All of a sudden a thick wall of flame will leap upwards

When they ask for proof from the Northerners.

The line of latitude '45 degrees' north runs pretty much plumb through the centre of Baghdad, which could indeed, back in 2003, have been construed as 'the great new city', given the enormous amount of building work undertaken, since the Gulf War of 1991, at the behest of the vainglorious Saddam Hussein. We know Nostradamus means the northern rather than the southern latitudes because of his mention of 'Normans', in line 4, which was a common euphemism at the time for those from the north.

It is certainly true that, for an unconscionably long time, Saddam Hussein, suffering, no doubt, from Dictator Denial Syndrome, chose to believe that the US and their British allies ('the Northerners') would not attack Baghdad itself – rather as Hitler once believed that Churchill would not declare war on Germany, and Stalin once believed that Hitler would honour the Nazi/Soviet non-aggression pact. The US then used what they called 'shock and awe' tactics on 20 March, and great walls of flame did indeed 'leap upwards' from all around Baghdad city, in a massive display of military firepower. The initial campaign was formally declared over by President Bush on 1 May 2003, paving the way for the much longer and more prickly transition towards a peaceful democracy.

SUMMARY

Saddam Hussein, playing a dangerous game of brinkmanship, finds his bluff called. Baghdad is bombed, and his regime is ended.

US/IRAQ WAR IV

Le gros mastin de cité deschassé

Sera fasché de l'etrange alliance

Apres aux champs avoir le cerf chassé

Le lous et l'ours se donront defiance.

ʊ

The great hound is driven from the city

Importuned by the foreign alliance

The stag is harried from the field

The wolf and the bear will defy each other.

The 'great hound' is Saddam Hussein, driven from his city, Baghdad, by the 'foreign alliance' of the United States and the United Kingdom, and finally captured, in December 2003, living six feet underground, in a hole. The image of the hole leads us to an amusing clue hidden inside this bestiary of a quatrain, for the 'stag' is a traditional symbol of Christ, and stems from its habit (according to Pliny's *Natural History*) of drawing serpents, by its breath, from their burrows, and then trampling them to death.

We also know that the ancient Christian community in Iraq (represented by the 'stag') is being driven out of the country to eventual extinction, further deepening the animal revocations. The 'bear', needless to say, is Russia, and the 'wolf' (an animal traditionally dedicated to Odin, the giver of victory) is the US. These two powers are facing off over Iraq and its oil reserves, with the US accusing Russia of illegally annexing the privatized oil company, Yukos, and Russia riposting with accusations that the US was only interested in liberating Iraq for its own long-term energy needs. So, alongside the animals, we can now add a bevy of fossils to further fuel Nostradamus's menagerie.

SUMMARY

Saddam Hussein is discovered hiding in a hole, like an animal. His fall will not be the end of the story, however. It will trigger further disasters, including the destruction of what remains of the ancient Christian community in Iraq.

Author's note: In hindsight, this quatrain may be seen as even more prescient, as now ISIS/ISIL are seeking to destroy not only the ancient Christian communities in Iraq, but also those of the Yazidis.

AUNG SAN SUU KYI & BURMA'S MILITARY JUNTA

DATE

2003 ONWARDS

QUATRAIN

4 / 41

Gymnique sexe captive par hostaige

Viendra de nuit custodes decevoyr:

Le chef du camp deceu par son langaige:

Lairra a la gente, sera piteux a voyr.

ॶ

A captive of the female sex

Will come by night; her guards will be deceived

The leader, angered by her tongue

Hands her to the people; it will be pitiful to see.

The most famous female political prisoner of the twenty-first century, and winner of the Nobel Peace Prize in 1991, is Burma's Aung San Suu Kyi. Elected leader of Burma (Myanmar) by a landslide victory in 1990, she has suffered house arrest in Rangoon (Yangon) on three separate occasions – for six years from 1989 to 1995; for a further twenty months until May 2002; and then from May 2003.

The military junta that has ruled Burma from 1962 is, indeed, 'angered by her tongue', and her guards have been 'deceived' into imprisoning her against the will of the people. Nostradamus foretells a time when she will be handed back to the people, triggering a tragedy. Whether this will be in the form of a civil war, or an assassination, is unclear.

A third possibility does arise, however, which would see her 'handing back to the people' as the trigger for a different sort of 'pitiful' event – that of the timely end of one of the few remaining totalitarian regimes in the region through the forces of mass insurrection.

SUMMARY

This quatrain, which I originally wrote and commentated on in 2005 (the text is exact), looked forward to the time when Aung San Suu Kyi, the elected president of Burma, would be released from house arrest.

Author's note: Aung San Suu Kyi was, in fact, released on 13 November 2010, proving that the quatrain was stunningly accurate. Nostradamus naysayers, therefore, whose stock-in-trade often consists of claims that not a single one of Nostradamus's prophecies for the future has ever been shown to be correct after the event – in other words a prophecy for the immediate future, formally published ahead of the event it predicts, being proved right retrospectively – now have a considerable amount of egg on their faces. A brief look at some of the other prophecies contained in this book (originally published in 2006 and updated in 2010) and dealing with the immediate future, should further reinforce the 'Nostradamus effect'.

TSUNAMI I

26 DECEMBER 2004

1/29

Quand le poisson, terrestre et aquatique,

Par forte vague au gravier sera mis,

Sa forme étrange suave et horrifique

Par mer aux murs bien tort enemies.

℧

When fish, both land and sea-based

Are thrown onshore by strong waves

Their strangely smooth, yet horrifying appearance

Will make of the twisted walls our enemy.

The force of the floods Nostradamus is describing will be powerful enough to drive maritime fish into the cities. The terrible deluge which caused their coming will mean that the ancient city 'walls', together with the 'walls' of people's houses, originally built to protect them, will now become threats. His accurate description of a tidal wave, or tsunami, as 'strangely smooth', is all the more haunting because such a concept would have been entirely outside his own experience.

The image of the smooth walls of water suddenly turning into a threat recall to mind the younger Pliny's letters to Tacitus (Epistle vi 16, 20), and his description of the tidal waves which struck Herculaneum after the eruption of Vesuvius, in August 79 AD. As well as destroying Pompeii and Stabiae, the monstrous waves also killed his uncle, the elder Pliny, whose name the former Publius Caecilius Secundus then took through adoption. A similar earthquake, magnitude 9.0 on the Richter scale, occurred off the west coast of Sumatra, Indonesia, at 00.58.33 UTC, on 26 December 2004, at the interface of the Indian and Burma plates. Maritime fish were, indeed, found on dry land after the disaster, and the 'walls' of the shifting tectonic plates did, undeniably, become our 'enemy'.

SUMMARY

A tsunami wave, triggered by a massive underwater earthquake, will ravage Indonesia and the surrounding areas.

Author's note: This extraordinary description of a tsunami perfectly correlates with the great Boxing Day 2004 Indian Ocean tsunami, which killed 230,000 people in fourteen countries, and devastated vast areas of Indonesia, Sri Lanka, India and Thailand.

DEATH OF POPE
JOHN PAUL II

DATE
2 APRIL 2005

QUATRAIN
8 / 46

Pol mensolee mourra trois lieus du Rosne

Fuis les deux prochains tarasc destrois

Car Mars fera le plus horrible trosne

De coq et d'aigle de France, freres trois.

℧

The celibate Pole (Paul) will die in three places in Rome

The next two flee the oppressive monster

Because Mars will occupy the papal throne

For the cock and the eagle of France, three brothers.

Nostradamus was particularly fond of predicting the deaths of popes, and here is his prediction of the death of Pope John Paul II (Karol Wojtyla), or 'the celibate Pole', at exactly 19.37 hours GMT, on Saturday 2 April 2005. The pope did, indeed, die in 'three places in Rome': his private apartments at the Vatican; in St Peter's Square, when his death was announced to the crowds; and in the crypt of St Peter's Basilica, where he is now buried. In addition, the Italian authorities immediately declared 'three' days of national mourning. The significance of the word 'three' is reiterated in line 4, with the 'three brothers'. Man is, of course, threefold, with the body, the soul and the spirit, and his enemies, too, are threefold, consisting of the world, the flesh and the devil. Even the Christian Graces are threefold, in Faith, Hope and Charity, and there are three sections of the Bible – the Old Testament, the New Testament and the Apocrypha. 'Three' is the perfect number, according to Pythagoras, symbolic of a beginning, a middle and an end, and three wise kings, Melchior, Gaspar and Balthazar, visited the infant Jesus in the stable. The Magi (the 'three brothers' in line 4) is taken, in Camoëns's *Lusiad*, to mean the same as the Indian word Brahmin, and we know that Brahma was one of the three beings created to assist in the creation of the world – thus proving the interconnectedness of every myth, every dogma, and every theocracy under the sun.

The 'oppressive monster', Tarascon, part lion, part crocodile, was tamed by Saint Martha, the patron saint of housewives, and she is traditionally shown with a bunch of keys at her girdle, symbolically equating to the papal keys of St Peter. The power of the keys (Matthew xvi. 19) is the supreme authority vested in the pope as the successor to St Peter, and one cannot help wondering if the next two popes who flee the 'oppressive monster' are not in fact fleeing the threat of female emancipation within the Catholic Church, as personified by St Martha? Either way, Mars, the god of war (but also of divine fortitude, the guardian power of Christianity) appears to occupy the papal throne for the period of these two papacies, and as both the cock and the eagle are traditionally viewed as male icons, as are the 'three brothers' of the Magi, so it seems likely that the traditional teachings of the Catholic Church will ultimately prevail.

SUMMARY

Following the death of Pope John Paul II, the next two popes will continue along the conservative path he blazed, opposing women priests, contraception and abortion.

Author's note: This quatrain, too, has been proved true, in that the two popes directly following John Paul II (popes Benedict XVI and Francis) have largely continued Pope John Paul II's conservative policies.

NEW ORLEANS FLOODS

AUGUST/SEPTEMBER 2005

3/84

La grand cité sera bien desolee,

Des habitans un seul n'y demoura

Mur, sexe, temple et vierge violee,

Par fer, feu, peste, canon peuple mourra.

༽

The great city will be laid to waste

Not even one inhabitant will remain

Walls, women, churches and virgins are violated

People will die by knife, fire, plague and gunshot.

Katrina, a Category Five hurricane, began her handiwork in New Orleans (a city whose 480,000 population was two thirds black, and in which forty per cent of children lived below the poverty line) on Monday 29 August 2005. Within just two days, eighty per cent of the urban area was ten feet under water, following the destruction of the levees built to contain Lake Pontchartrain, and rioting, looting, arson and rape had broken out across the Crescent City, pending the imposition of martial law. And Nostradamus, here in quatrain 3/84, describes the situation exactly, right down to the evacuation of every single inhabitant of the city ('not even one inhabitant will remain'); to the knifings and rapes amongst the 60,000 refugees in the New Orleans Superdome stadium, including the violation of a seven-year-old girl – Nostradamus's *vierge*; to the killing of five looters on the Danziger Bridge; and, finally, to the infections arising from the pollution of the flood waters by waste toxins, dead bodies and sewage-related bacteria.

SUMMARY

The great Mississippi River flood of 1927 and the 2005 New Orleans, Alabama, and Mississippi Delta flood, with its 140mph winds and twenty-five-foot storm surges covering a 90,000 square-mile area – the same size as the United Kingdom – were the two greatest natural disasters in US history. Go to 9/48 – 2048 [US Hurricanes/Global Warming III] for the next great US environmental disaster.

CRISIS IN THE PROTESTANT CHURCH

Dans le temple clos le foudre y entrera,

Les citadins dedans leur fort grevez

Chevaux, boeufs, hommes, l'onde mur touchera,

Par faim, soif, soubs les plus faibles armez.

ʊ

Lightning will enter the sealed church

The people inside will be deeply aggrieved

Horses, cattle, men, the ripened wave will touch them all

Due to hunger and thirst, even the weakest will arm themselves.

A *temple*, in Old French, referred specifically to a Protestant church. Given this fact, it now appears that there will be a crisis, sometime in 2006, undermining the vacuum which now exists inside the Protestant convocation. This has been on the cards for some time ('ripened wave'), and will affect everything and everyone to do with the Church ('horses, cattle, men'). Sidelined, even the female members of the Church ('the weakest') will join in the argument on the side of change. Given all this, and the index date of 2006, one's thoughts inevitably turn towards the question of homosexual bishops, and the schisms beginning to appear inside the global Anglican community as a result of the appointment of the Reverend Canon Gene Robinson as its first openly gay bishop, of New Hampshire, in August 2003. Further to this, of course, is the question of female bishops, and to the unrest their ordination will create amongst hardliners. The telling image of the women arming themselves, in line 4, may, of course, simply refer to the assumption, by female aspirants, of the bishop's crosier, and serves us with additional remarkable testimony to Nostradamus's predictive powers.

SUMMARY

The Anglican Church will be thrown into disarray by the perpetual argument over gay clergy and female bishops. There is the distinct possibility of a permanent schism between the conservative and the liberal elements of the synod, which may result in the Church splitting into two separate congregations.

Author's note: This prediction was written in 2005, based on my reading of quatrain 3/6, and Nostradamus's own index date. In the intervening period the quatrain has been proved 100 per cent true, with particular reference to the 18 June 2006 elevation of Katherine Jefferts Schori to presiding Bishop of the United States Episcopal Church, making her the first woman to reach the level of primate in any of the world's Anglican churches (my book was first published on 15 February 2006). The schism begun by the elevation of Schori and the openly gay Bishop of New Hampshire Gene Robinson duly came to a head in the 2008 Anglican General Synod, held under the aegis of the Archbishop of Canterbury.

In July 2014, the General Synod of the Church of England voted to allow the ordination of women bishops and on 26 January 2015 the Right Reverend Libby Lane became the first ever female bishop when she was made Bishop of Stockport. These developments have, as the quatrain above suggested back in 2005, caused an ever-widening rift between 'conservative' and 'liberal' clerics.

POPE BENEDICT XVI

12 SEPTEMBER 2006

5 / 74

De sang Troyé naistra coeur Germanique,

Qu'il deviendra en si haulte puissance:

Hors chassera gent estrange Arabique,

Tournant l'eglise en pristine preeminence.

ও

A German heart is born of Trojan blood

He will wield such power

That he will chase away the foreign Arabs

Returning the church to her immaculate preeminence.

Well, in the light of the accession of Bavarian-born Joseph Alois Ratzinger to the papal throne on 24 April 2005, as number 265 of an as yet unbroken line (and the first German-born pope in 1,000 years, if one bars the brief 1522–23 reign of Dutch/German Adrian VI), and in the light of the comments the newly fledged Pope Benedict XVI is reported to have made about Islam on 12 September 2006, Nostradamus appears to have hit the nail squarely on the head once again. Born at Marktl am Inn, the former Cardinal Ratzinger (and Archbishop of Munich and Friesing) quoted from a little-known (outside ecclesiastical circles, at least, one supposes) *Dialogue Held with a Certain Persian, the Worthy Mouterizes, in Anakara of Galatia*: 'Show me just what Muhammad brought that was new and there you will find things only evil and inhuman, such as his command to spread by the sword the faith he preached.'

The pope was apparently quoting the Catholic theologian and nonsectarian translator of the Koran into German Professor Adel Theodore Khoury; who was commenting on the discussions held between the aforementioned Mouterizes and Byzantine Emperor Manuel II Palaiologos, in 1391, in which Manuel made the point that warfare in the name of God (in the sense of suggesting a 'lack of reason') was contrary to God's will. Mouterizes had apparently countered by suggesting that, in Islam, God is considered to transcend so-called 'rationality', even to the extent – according to the Andalucian-born Islamic scholar Ibn Hazm (994–1064) – 'of not being bound by his own word'. This fundamental difference (in whether God is, or is not, bound by so-called rationality) is highlighted, according to Pope

Benedict, by the concept of Islamic 'forced conversion' or Jihad (anathema to modern Catholics, although not, one recalls, to their predecessors in what is now Latin America).

For this reason, just as Nostradamus infers, it may constitute the one insurmountable Chinese Wall that prevents the two religions from ever fully understanding the bases of each other's doctrines.

One final (only marginally) amusing note: Sheik Abu Saqer, leader of Gaza's Jihadia Salafiya Outreach Movement, unconsciously drew together a number of Nostradamus's main quatrain images in his enraged response to the pope's words:

> *The call for so-called dialogue by this little racist Pope is a Trojan Horse... the only Christian-Muslim dialogue that is acceptable is one in which all religions agree to convert to Islam.*

SUMMARY

Nostradamus gives us a German-born pope who galvanizes the Catholic Church against what he considers to be the more extreme and unacceptable aspects of the Islamic faith, with an emphasis on the peaceful and rational links between 'People of the Book'.

ASSASSINATION OF A WORLD LEADER

DATE
2006–2008

QUATRAIN
10/26

Le successeur vengera son beau frere,
Occupera regne souz umbre de vengeance,
Occis ostacle son sang mort vitupere,
Long temps Bretaigne tiendra avec la France.

ひ

The successor will avenge his handsome brother

He will take over the realm under cover of vengeance

The obstacle slain, his dead blood seethes

Britain and France will hold together for a long time.

Given the tenor of the first two lines, in which 'vengeance' and the 'taking over of a realm' are mentioned, it seems that Nostradamus is referring to a major political assassination in this quatrain. This reading is further strengthened by the reference to Britain and France in line 4, suggesting that the events due to unfold have worldwide implications. It is tempting to assume that Nostradamus is referring to someone's brother-in-law (*beau frere*), and not to a 'handsome brother', in line 1, but the reading would be a false one. The words *beau* and *frere* are categorically unlinked, whereas they would undoubtedly be linked or hyphenated if brother-in-law were the intended meaning.

A possible clue to the identity of the handsome brother lies in line 2, in the words *souz umbre* – 'under cover'. Nostradamus is referring to a place where one would seek protection when out in the wild: e.g. a under a 'bush'. Once this is grasped, the quatrain becomes a little easier to unravel, although it is still impossible to be entirely sure which world leader (with a brother already holding high office) will be the eventual assassination target.

One of many possible targets, of course, might be US president George W. Bush. In such an imagined scenario, Nostradamus would appear to be positing that the president's brother – in this purely exemplary case it would be Jeb Bush, already a twice-elected Governor of Florida – would be voted in, by an outraged US electorate, in his place. Nostradamus then goes on to picture the outraged brother of the victim avenging his 'handsome' brother, but by actions that would so alienate his country's erstwhile ally,

Britain, that it is driven to align itself with France (in this case standing for the whole of the European Union), an alliance which will, unlike those of the past, hold together for a long time.

SUMMARY

An attempt is made to assassinate a powerful world leader. Should the attempt be successful, the brother of the world leader will be elected in his stead. He will take revenge for his brother's death, and this will so alienate his country's main ally, Britain, that it will be forced to turn its back on its old alliances, and align itself with the newly emerging European superstate, personified, in this instance, by France.

Author's note: As with quatrain 3/6 – 2006: Crisis in the Protestant Church, this quatrain appeared, verbatim, in the first edition of this book (published in February 2006). The prediction itself was written in 2005, based on my reading of quatrain 10/26. In the interim, Benazir Bhutto, undoubtedly a 'World Leader' of the first magnitude, was assassinated by unknown elements on 27 December 2007.

In retrospect, therefore, my assumption that the assassinated individual mentioned in lines 1 and 2 was of necessity a man was potentially a false one, although the London *Daily Telegraph* of 19 July 2008 did carry the following report, which I quote verbatim: 'Israel has arrested six Arab men over an alleged plot to assassinate President George W. Bush, according to Shin Bet, the Israeli internal security service.' It's interesting, too, that George Bush's brother, Jeb Bush, looks likely to be one of the Republican contenders for president in 2016.

The 'handsome brother' in line 1 is now clearly one of the two assassinated brothers of Benazir Bhutto. The first, twenty-seven-year-old Shahnawaz Bhutto, was found dead in Nice, on 18 July 1985 – poisoning was suspected. The second, Murtaza Bhutto, was shot and killed on 20 September 1996, in a police ambush in Karachi.

Notable, too, is the fact that the assassinated Benazir Bhutto's husband, Asif Ali Zardari, became the twelfth president of Pakistan on 9 September 2008. In the light of this event, the first line of the quatrain, 'the successor will avenge his handsome brother', takes on even more significance, in the sense that both of Benazir Bhutto's assassinated brothers were brothers by marriage of President Zardari.

AFTERMATH OF POPE JOHN PAUL II'S DEATH

Apparoistra vers le Septentrion,

Non loin de Cancer l'estoille chevelue:

Suze, Sienne, Boece Eretrion,

Mourra de Rome grand, la nuict disperue.

There will be seen, towards the north

Not far from Cancer, a beard-trailing star

Susa, Sienna, Bocche, Etruria

When the great one dies in Rome, the night will disappear.

Horace Tuttle was the first person to discover comet 41P/Tuttle-Giacobini-Kresak, way back in 1858. '41P', as we shall call it from here on in, began retrograding through Orion in 2006, and then, just as Nostradamus predicted, it swung northwards, cutting through Taurus, Gemini, Cancer, Leo and Virgo. It at first seems likely, given the contents of this quatrain ('when the great one dies in Rome'), and its index date of 6, that Nostradamus was initially a year out in his prediction of Pope John Paul II's death [which is really not too bad a result, come to think of it, after 450 years – *see* 8/46 – 2005: Death of Pope John Paul II], but in retrospect it seems that Nostradamus may have been dealing with the aftermath of the pope's death, and its effect on the Catholic Church.

The image that 'the night will disappear' is an interesting one, and causes one to wonder whether Nostradamus isn't talking about the reinstatement of the Tridentine Mass as a so-called Extraordinary Form of the Roman Rite, a position it had not held since 1962? This neatly takes us back to Orion ('*Septentrion*'), and good old 41P.

The mighty hunter Orion, noted for his manly beauty, was blinded by Oenopion, but Vulcan (the great cuckold), in an uncharacteristic fit of pity, sent Cedalion down to guide him back through his old hunting grounds (the symbolic reversion to old and tried forms of behaviour). Orion's sight was eventually restored by the exposure of his eyeballs to the sun – 'the night', in other words, was made to 'disappear' – but the near-ubiquitous Diana (*cave feminam* – remember the moral of Aristophanes's *Thesmophoriazusae*, a.k.a. *Men Beware women?*) ended up by killing him, and he was made into his very own constellation, through which 41P retrograded in 2006. And thereby hangs a tail.

SUMMARY

A follow-on to 8/46 – 2005: Death of Pope John Paul II, this quatrain would appear to be highlighting the raising of the Tridentine Mass to 'Extraordinary Status' by Pope John Paul's successor, Pope Benedict XVI – ergo Nostradamus's telling image of 'night being turned back into day'.

NORTH KOREAN CRISIS

Les fugitifs, feu du ciel sus les piques.

Conflict prochain des corbeaux s'esbatans,

De terre on crie aide secours celiques,

Quand pres des murs seront les combatans.

༐

Fire from above will spike the fugitives

Soon the ravens will start bickering

Earth-bound cries beg heaven for assistance

When the fighters approach the walls.

In Egyptian hieroglyphics, a 'raven' symbolizes contention. In later times, it was considered a bird of ill omen, probably due to its habit of following armies and ravening on the dead bodies left in their wake. Throughout ancient history, bickerings between ravens and crows were considered as prognostications of terrible events – Jovianus Pontanus tells of such an event before the battle of Beneventum, and Nicetas speaks of a similar occurrence before the Scythians invaded Thrace. The great orator Cicero was forewarned of his death by the fluttering of ravens in his room, and the Athenian Oracle declared that 'ravens bear the characters of Saturn ... and have a very early perception of the bad disposition of that planet.'

As to the identity of the walled city in line 4, one is forced back to line 1, and the word *pique*, which can have multiple meanings. The obvious ones are 'pike', and to be 'stung' or 'spiked'. In Old French, though, a *piqué* was a quilted waistcoat, such as was traditionally worn by the Chinese or the Koreans. The word 'walls' in line 4 cements the Korean, rather than the Chinese reading, however. In the *Annals of the Three Kingdoms*, written by Il Jon in the late thirteenth century, it is said that Tangun Wanggom set up his capital at Pyongyang Walls, and named his country Korea.

SUMMARY

North Korea will refuse to accede to the West's demands over clarification of its nuclear capacity. A crisis will be triggered which may lead to war.

Author's note: As with quatrain 3/6 – 2006: Crisis in the Protestant Church, and 10/26 – 2006: Assassination of a World Leader, this quatrain appeared, verbatim, in the first edition of this book (published in February 2006). The prediction itself was written in 2005, based on my reading of quatrain 3/7, and has since proved to be a correct one, as North Korea conducted its first ever nuclear test on 9 October 2006, triggering the expected crisis. The crisis came to a head in early 2007 (*see* index date), and was happily defused later that same year when North Korea backed down from its nuclear programme in the face of considerable worldwide pressure. Despite its destruction of a cooling tower on 27 June 2008, North Korea still retains the capacity to reignite its nuclear programme at very short notice indeed. Recent problems over the 2014 Hollywood movie *The Interview*, which saw North Korea briefly threatening war, adds still further credibility to this powerful quatrain.

FINANCIAL MELTDOWN/ CREDIT CRUNCH

Les simulachres d'or & argent enflez,

Qu'apres le rapt au lac furent gettez

Au desouvert estaincts tous & troublez.

Au marbre escript prescripz intergetez.

ʊ

Fake versions of gold and silver multiply

Such that after the abduction they are thrown into the lake

On their rediscovery, global exhaustion and trouble

All debts are voided.

This is a categorical depiction of the 2008 world financial crisis, right down to Nostradamus's memorable phrase, 'all debts are voided', with its inevitable evocation of the US sub-prime mortgage debacle. It describes 2008's global financial meltdown to a T, triggered by the use of artificial replacements for cash – e.g. credit cards, national debt, commodity speculation, hedge funds, and a raft of other dubious financial instruments. As well as abduction, '*rapt*' can also be used in the sense of a rape. Following the rape of the financial markets, therefore, and the worldwide collapse of fake monetary objects, all debts between nation states are put into question. Whether this will also apply to individual debt is a touch more debatable. [*see* 2/28 – 2008: Religious Revival, for an alternative reading]

SUMMARY

It is the ninetieth year after the great 1929 Wall Street stock market crash, and Nostradamus is predicting another equally catastrophic event. This time, the crash will mirror the collapse of spiritual values throughout the Western world.

Author's note: I originally dated this quatrain as 2028 in the 2006 edition of this book, but in the light of recent occurrences, and given the index date of 8/28, it seems only sensible to shift the quatrain to 2008, where it tallies perfectly with the financial meltdown which beset so many of the world's economies in that year.

RELIGIOUS REVIVAL

Le penultime du surnom du prophete

Prendra Diane pour son iour & repos:

Loing vaguera par frenetique teste,

Et delivrant un grand peuple d'impos.

෪

The last but one holder of the prophet's name

Will take Diana for his day and for his rest

He will wander far with his head in a frenzy

Delivering a great people from financial subjugation.

PREDICTION

This quatrain is particularly interesting given its index-date link with 8/28 – 2008 [Financial Meltdown/Credit Crunch]. Both deal, quite clearly, with taxes, debt, and financial crisis, but this one has a spiritual dimension as well, and forces us back to a second possible reading of 8/28, in which 'fake versions of gold and silver' become false religious icons. The Koran claims that there have been 200,000 prophets, but that only six are significant, in that they have brought in new laws and dispensations. These six are Adam, Noah, Abraham, Moses, Jesus and Muhammad. A prophet is, technically speaking, one who announces the divine will, and stems originally from the ancient Greek, although the meaning is strictly Hebrew. The Hebrews themselves recognized many prophets, and the Gautama Buddha, of course, would also come under this category, though he encapsulated the Light, rather than merely interpreting it. Nostradamus, though a scryer and seer, would certainly not have considered himself amongst their number, however.

The Roman goddess Diana's day is Monday, as she took over, amongst other things, the post of goddess of the moon from the Greek goddess Artemis. The Roman habit of filching things from the Greeks rather muddies the water where Diana is concerned, but she was also supposed to promote the union of communities, and to represent plebeians and slaves. In France Lunedi was the saint associated with Mondays, and it became, in consequence, a day of rest for workers, further cementing the links in the first two lines of the quatrain.

SUMMARY

Following the great financial crash of 2008, a spiritual vacuum can be detected throughout Western society. This triggers a gradual return to organized religion, and a concomitant revival in spirituality and religious practice.

ADVANCE WARNING OF THIRD ANTICHRIST

DATE
2010

QUATRAIN
10/10

Tasche de murdre enormes adulteres
Grand ennemi de tout le genre humain
Que sera pire qu'ayeulx, oncles ne peres
En fer, feu, eau, sanguin et inhumain.

℧

Stained with mass murder and adultery

This great enemy of humanity

Will be worse than any man before him

In steel, fire, water, bloody and monstrous.

This is an early portent of the coming of the third Antichrist, echoing the warning tones of St John the Evangelist in I John 2. xvii–xviii, even down to St John's concept of the transitory lust for material things, as postulated in 'And the world passeth away, and the lust thereof': Nostradamus certainly doesn't pull any punches here, describing the future depredations of the Antichrist as 'worse than any man before him', which, if one considers the first two Antichrists to be either Napoleon and Hitler, or Stalin and Hitler, depending on which reading one adheres to, is really saying something. Go to 7/32 & 2/32 – 2032, 3/34 – 2034, 3/35 – 2035, 9/36 – 2036, 10/75 – 2075 and 8/77 – 2077 for a further taste of what lies in store for the next few generations.

SUMMARY

The third Antichrist will be even more destructive than his two predecessors, and the results of his actions will darken and distort the history of the twenty-first century.

GLOBAL WARMING I

DATE
2011

QUATRAIN
5 / 11

Mer par solaires sevre ne passera

Ceux de Venus tiendront toute l'Affrique

Leur regne plus Saturne n'occupera

Et changera la part Asiatique.

℧

The sea, chastened by the sun, will no longer pass

The heat of Venus will harry all of Africa

Saturn will no longer measure its reign

The Asiatic part will change.

The Suez Canal will begin to dry up due to global warming, bringing Asia closer to Africa. The heat of Venus, second planet from the sun (and the one that approaches nearest to the earth and is most similar to us in size and density) will devastate the African continent. When one considers, for a moment, that the surface temperatures of Venus are in the region of 460°C, Nostradamus's image is a powerful one. Saturn appears here in the guise of Kronos (Time), with his relentless sickle to hand, the implication being that this is a permanent change – the end of a Golden Age, even – when the earth brought forth abundantly, and without the need for tilling. This reading is further reinforced by the fact that Saturn was, on the one hand, the Roman god of agriculture, and on the other, in his guise as the youngest of the Titans, the enthusiastic devourer of his own children.

SUMMARY

The effects of global warming will start to be felt in Africa, that most vulnerable of continents. There will be famine and drought, and, in some places, even cannibalism.

DANGERS TO JOHN PAUL II'S SUCCESSOR, BENEDICT XVI

QUATRAIN
4 / 11

Celui qu'aura gouvert de la grand cappe,

Sera induict à quelques cas patrer

Les douzes rouges viendront fouiller la nappe.

Soubz meutre, meutre se viendra perpetrer.

ℭ

He who governs with the papal cloak

Will be induced to act as shepherd

The twelve red ones will come to bury his communion cloth

Under cover of murder, murder will be done.

The Catholic Church has harboured murderers in its ranks before. Indeed, many people still continue to allege that Pope John Paul I was done away with by elements of the Curia (the Church Administration) after only thirty-four days in office, in September 1978, and that he was killed precisely because he had just completed, but not yet publicized, dismissal orders for a list of highly placed opponents of change. This time the new pope is being pushed to lead from the back, as a 'shepherd' does, by twelve massively influential cardinals. The image of the burial of the 'communion cloth' in line 3 is a worrying one, and its correlation to the 'papal cloak' in line 1 is categorical. The pope's life is definitely in danger.

SUMMARY

After a period of acting simply as the shepherd of the Church, Pope Benedict XVI decides to stretch his wings a little. There will be a threat to his life.

Author's note: With the benefit of hindsight (I am writing this note in 2015), Nostradamus seems even more prescient when he talks of the pope (in this case Pope Benedict XVI) being 'induced to act as shepherd'. As we now know, Pope Benedict announced his resignation on 11 February 2013, citing 'a lack of strength in mind and body' (the 'threat to his life'). This correlates perfectly with Nostradamus's extraordinary image of the twelve cardinals ('red ones') 'coming to bury his communion cloth' (meaning that, by personal choice, Pope Benedict will no longer be able to give communion). He will, however, act 'as shepherd' in guiding his successor, Pope Francis.

DEATH OF A POPE I

Esleu en Pape, d'esleu sera mocqué

Subit soudain esmeu prompt et timide

Par trop bon doulz à mourir provocqué

Crainte estainte la nuit de sa mort guide.

༚

An elected Pope, mocked by his electors

Suddenly acts, though briefly and timidly

He is killed for being too good

He will fear the death of his guide, the night he dies.

The 'electors' in line 1 are the College of Cardinals, and not the members of the Catholic Church, who have no say whatsoever in who leads them. Uncharacteristically, and unilaterally, the pope acts, after a long period of entropy. His advisers are horrified. Though well-meaning, he is perceived to be endangering the guiding principles of Catholic dogma. On the night that he dies, the pope is already anticipating Godlessness, encapsulated in the symbolical 'death of his guide', God.

SUMMARY

Following the threat to his life mentioned in the last quatrain, Pope Benedict XVI acts, though in an uncharacteristic manner. Either as the result of an earlier injury, or after a fresh attempt on his life, the pope dies.

Author's note: Again, in retrospect (I am writing this in 2015) the pope's 'death' here may be seen as a symbolical one. One pope 'dies' so that the other one may 'rise' – something virtually unprecedented in the Catholic Church (before Benedict, no pope had resigned in almost 600 years).

PRINCESS DIANA
& DODI FAYED

2012

9 / 12

Le tant d'argent de Diane et Mercure

Les simulacres au lac seront trouvez,

Le figulier cherchant argille neufve

Lui et les siens d'or seront abbrevez.

೪ೡ

Despite all the money of Diana and Mercury

Their empty shadows will be found at the lake

For the potter in search of new clay

He and his people will be drenched with gold.

Diana, Princess of Wales, and her lover, Dodi Fayed (son of Mohammed al Fayed, owner of Harrods, London's world-famous department store) were killed in a car crash in Paris, early on the morning of 31 August 1997 – a moment when neither their fame nor their fortune could help them, as Nostradamus so clearly delineates in line 1. Diana's brother, Lord Spencer, oversaw the building of a water park at their natal Althorp Estate in honour of her life, and Diana's 'empty shadow' is indeed buried on an island, on the lake, with Dodi's shadow forever bound up with hers.

Dodi Fayed is associated with Mercury, in line 1, for Mercury was the Roman god of trade, and both Dodi and his father owed their fortunes to commerce. The last two lines are more of a mystery, though. Ancient American Indian lore has it that we are all made of clay, and that Manitou simply baked the white man for too short a period, and the black man for too long a period – the red man he baked just right. This concept (with the usual variations, depending on self-interest) runs through many religions, and Romans ix. 21, is particularly succinct on the matter: 'Hath not the potter power over the clay, of the same lump to make one vessel unto honour, and another unto dishonour?'

The concept of gold inevitably leads us back to Midas, King of Phrygia, and his request to the gods that everything he touch be turned to gold. Lady Diana Spencer made a similar request by marrying Prince Charles, heir to the British throne, and so, in his way, did Dodi Fayed, when he took up with the golden-haired Diana. Perhaps the real potter Nostradamus was referring to was Demetrius, a silversmith of Ephesus, who specialized in making gold and silver shrines for the temple of Diana? When idolatry was in danger of castigation by the simplicity of the Apostle Paul's Gospel, all the silversmiths, including Demetrius, came out on strike, and, for the space of two hours (as Acts xix. 24–28 tells us) they shouted 'Great is Diana of the Ephesians!' We all know what happened next. There may be a message there for all idolaters.

SUMMARY

Nostradamus muses on the briefness of celebrity. Following the deaths of Princess Diana and Dodi Fayed in a car crash in 1997, all the money and fame in the world are no longer of use to them. All that remains, fifteen years on, are their empty shadows in the memorial water park at Althorp.

NUCLEAR FISSION

Par fouldre en l'arche or et argent fondu

De deux captifs l'un l'autre mangera

De la cité le plus grand estendu

Quand submergée la classe nagera.

&

Gold and silver are fused by the ark's devastating power

The one is cannibalized by the other

The leader of the city is stretched

When the fleet travels underwater.

The word *arche* has many possible connotations, ranging from alchemy (*archée*: the central fire of life), to Noah's Ark, to the Ark of the Covenant, to the concept of *étre hors de l'arche* (to be beyond the pale of the Church). When twinned with the image of a 'fleet which travels underwater', we are inevitably led towards the concept of a submarine, driven by nuclear fission – an unholy power, in other words, strong enough to fuse the disparate elements of dark and light, and which threatens the security of a great city. The Ark of the Covenant, as well as being the repository of the two great tablets of the Decalogue, did, of course, also act as a safeguard in times of war, a function now taken up by the rather more secular form of the nuclear submarine. Some maintain that the Ark is now lost, but others believe that it remains under permanent guard by a single monk who never ventures into the outside world, at a remote monastic church in Ethiopia.

SUMMARY
Nostradamus compares the power of nuclear fission to that of the Ark of the Covenant, with the first bringing materialistic darkness, and the second, spiritual light. Given the very real threat of Iran's potential nuclear capability, this quatrain must be seen as particularly prescient.

ABORTION DEBATE REIGNITES IN THE CATHOLIC CHURCH

DATE
2013

QUATRAIN
2 / 13

Le corps sans ame plus n'estre en sacrifice

Jour de la mort mis en nativité

L'esprit divin fera l'ame felice

Voyant le verbe en son eternité.

༒

The soul-less body will no longer be sacrificed

It will be born on the day of death

The divine spirit will make the soul happy

Seeing the eternal word.

This quatrain has traditionally been taken as a straightforward hymn to the resurrection, despite the categorical nature of line 1. The 'body without a soul', however, is that of an unborn child, and not that of a human being approaching death, which already has a soul. The philosopher Aristotle taught that the unborn foetus only becomes ensouled, in the case of a male child, after forty days in the womb, and in the case of a female child, after eighty days. The Catholic Church accepted Aristotle's opinion until 1621, when its own interpretation changed to one of cross-gender ensoulment at conception, echoing, curiously enough, Buddhist views on the subject. Both St Thomas and St Jerome, though, hardliners to a man, condemned abortion outright, despite its virtual non-appearance in the Bible [Exodus xxi, 22–23, for instance, saw it only as a fining offence, except in the case of the consequent death of the mother].

The Jewish religion reflects the Old Testament view (it should be remembered that Nostradamus was a Catholic Jew, and died in 1566, before the Catholic change of tack), and holds that a child is not ensouled in the womb, but only becomes 'human' when the head appears – at this point, even if the mother is endangered, the child must not be killed. Before that, no capital offence will have occurred. This view is so widespread that, to this day, women soldiers in the Israeli Defense Forces are entitled to two free abortions during the course of their two-year stint.

What Nostradamus appears to be postulating in this quatrain, however, is that abortion is fundamentally wrong, and that the destroyed foetus is ensouled at the moment of its death ('it will be born on the day of death'), a view reinforced by the next line which reiterates the concept of ensoulment as a means of enlightenment by the divine word. The implication, therefore, is that the Catholic view of the theocratic illegality of abortion will harden, rather than soften, during the rekindling of this debate, just as it hardened back in 1621.

SUMMARY

The abortion debate flares up again, this time within the Mother Church itself. The Church maintains its intractable line on the termination of an unborn foetus being tantamount to murder.

DEATH OF A POPE II

QUATRAIN
4 / 14

La mort subite du premier personnage
Aura changé et mis un autre au regne
Tost, tard venu à si haut et bas aage,
Que terre et mer faudre que on la craigne.

ℰℐ

The unexpected death of the first among many

Will create change, making another man leader

Soon, but also too late, a young man will attain high office

By land and sea he must be feared.

Following on from 10/12 – 2012 [Death of a Pope I], and 2/13 – 2013 [Abortion Debate Reignites in the Catholic Church], and anticipating the 2017 series of scandals in the Church covered in 3/17, 9/2 and 6/17, this quatrain deals with the accession of a new and younger pope to the Triple Crown. Why a pope, and not a president? Because only a pope, in the terms that Nostradamus would understand them, can be a *premier personnage*. Let us remind ourselves of what the Triple Crown represents: firstly, the Head of the Catholic, or Universal, Church; secondly, the Sole Arbiter of its rights; thirdly, the Sovereign Father of all the kings of the earth. That's pretty categorical, isn't it? The 'feared' in line 4 should be taken, in this context, in the same way that God-fearing used to be taken, i.e. as indicating obedience, rather than terror. Given all that, we now have a relatively young pope, taking over unexpectedly from a traditionalist pope (which we know from the Abortion Debate in 2/13). The scandals predicted three years later, in 2017, are now placed in their proper perspective.

SUMMARY

A relatively young pope has acceded to the Triple Crown. He is a liberal. Following more than thirty years of largely conservative rule, his election raises hackles amongst the remaining traditionalist cardinals.

Author's note: This quatrain appeared, verbatim, in the 2006 edition of this book. In the light of Pope Benedict's resignation ('a symbolical death') in 2013, Nostradamus's second line ('will create change, making another man leader') and the index date of 14, making him only one year out in 458, are stunningly accurate.

FAMINE RELIEF

D'où pensera faire venir famine,
De là viendra le rassasiement
L'oeil de la mer par avare canine
Pour de l'un l'autre donra huile, froment.

෯

From where they thought famine would come

Comes relief

The eyes of the sea are like a greedy dog's

One eye will provide oil, the other, wheat.

According to the United Nations Hunger Map for 2015 (the index date of this quatrain), there were in that year 795 million people – more than 10 per cent of the world's population – without enough to eat, and facing famine. Had this sort of data collection prevailed in Nostradamus's time, he would probably have found such a report unremarkable. Hunger in Europe was occasioned even by a single crop failure, and consecutive poor harvests brought certain famine. But in this prediction, the seer seems unusually optimistic for the distant future. He foresees a time where the sea, often cast as a threat [*see* 1/29 – 2004: Tsunami I], will finally break the pattern of famine. We will instead see the oceans as a resource expressed in the metaphor of the greedy dog's eyes summoning up oil and wheat – a notion perhaps of hungry populations experiencing eerie visions of energy and food production far ahead.

As to the relief of famine, Nostradamus's optimism was well-founded, in the long term. While poverty has always been recognized as a relative condition, there is now some agreement between nations that absolute poverty worldwide has been reduced more in the last 50 years than in all of the preceding 500.

SUMMARY

The world begins to find answers to famine. Nostradamus acknowledges the dangers inherent in a growing population and exhorts us to find sustainable resources by alternative means.

HILLARY CLINTON

2015

8 / 15

Vers Aquilon grands efforts par hommasse

Presque l'Europe et l'univers vexer,

Les deux eclypses mettra en telle chasse,

Et aux Pannons vie et mort renforcer.

૭૭

The masculine woman will exert herself to the north

She will annoy nearly all of Europe and the rest
of the world

Two failures will put her in such an imbalance

That both life and death will strengthen
eastern Europe.

Hillary Clinton announced her candidature for the US presidency in 2015, the index date of this quatrain. She won the Democrat nomination in July 2016 and was defeated in the November poll of that year. As a 'masculine woman' in Nostradamus's image she is projected not as unfeminine in person, but in the role she aspired to fulfil. Her two failures were to lose the election that would have made her the first woman leader of the 'free world' and, no less significantly, to make way for a candidate, Donald Trump, capable of causing annoyance everywhere, particularly in eastern Europe. This region is peculiarly sensitive to the United States' relationship with Russia, whose government might have undermined Mrs Clinton's election campaign. The Pannons referred to in the original quatrain were a tribal people of eastern Europe in Roman times, a region now corresponding to much of Austria, Greece, former Yugoslavia, Hungary, Bulgaria, Albania and parts of Turkey. Velleius Paterculus, historian and contemporary of Julius Caesar, thought the Pannons untrustworthy, and Ammianus, a soldier-historian of fourth-century Rome, made much of their cunning and versatility.

SUMMARY

Hillary Clinton's failure to become the first female president of the United States betokens upheaval among populations of eastern Europe comparable to the time of the western Roman empire.

Author's note: This quatrain appeared, verbatim, in the 2006 edition of this book. I think it fair to say that it is fully accurate, particularly if one realizes that I wrote my commentary back in 2005, a good ten years before the events spoken of in the quatrain.

ECOLOGICAL DISASTERS I

Faulx à l'estang joint vers le Sagitaire,

En son hault Auge de l'exaltation,

Peste, famine, mort de main militaire,

La siecle approche de renouvation.

Scythes in the mill-run, joining towards Sagittarius

In its high mill-course of exaltation

Plague, famine, and death through war

The century approaches its remaking.

Both *estang* and *auge* are milling terms, and we may assume that Nostradamus used them intentionally, to imply a grinding or milling process of ecological and alchemical change. 'Scythes', as well as implying death (a common image in fifteenth and sixteenth-century Tarot cards), would also, if taken literally, rust and become useless if thrown into a millpond. This is a direct image from the Revelation of St John the Divine 6. vi., describing the fourth of the four beasts seated before the throne of God, all of whom have eyes both before and behind them, and who are instrumental in the opening of the Seven Seals on the Day Of Wrath: 'And I heard a voice in the midst of the four beasts say, A measure of wheat for a penny, and three measures of barley for a penny; and see thou hurt not the oil and the wine.'

Sagitaire, in line 1, represents Sagittarius the archer, and he is the horseman revealed at the opening of the First Seal, by the beckoning of the first of the four beasts: 'And I saw, and behold a white horse; and he that sat on him had a bow;' [Revelations 6. ii.]. The upshot of the opening of the last of the Seven Seals is too abominable to contemplate, and we must take this quatrain as a warning, alongside its neighbours, 4/15 – 2015, 8/16 – 2016, and 1/17 – 2017, about the damage we are doing to our planet and to its climate.

SUMMARY

Another warning, by Nostradamus, of the wrong direction the world is taking.

ECOLOGICAL
DISASTERS II

Au lieu que Hieron feit sa nef fabriquer,

Si grand deluge sera et si subite,

Qu'on n'aura lieu ne terres s'atacquer

L'onde monter Fesulan Olympique.

In the place where Hero mourned

Such a great and sudden flood will occur

That there will be no land left to cling to

The waves will rise over Mount Olympus.

Most commentators take *Hieron*, in line 1, to be a cryptogram for Jason (of 'the Argonauts' fame), but this commentator begs to differ. It seems far more likely that Nostradamus meant Hero (in French: *Heron*), the priestess of Aphrodite who drowned herself in the Hellespont (now known as the Dardanelles) for love of Leander. Leander was from Abydos, a settlement on the opposite shore to that of Aphrodite's temple at Sestos. Each night, Leander would swim across the strait to be with his lover (just as Lord Byron swam across it many centuries later, in 1810, in honour of their love):

> He could, perhaps, have pass'd the Hellespont,
> As once (a feat on which ourselves we prided)
> Leander, Mr Ekenhead, and I did.
> > [Don Juan, Canto ii. St. 105]

Hero would guide Leander towards her by the light of a torch until, one night, a great wave reared up and swept him away. Inconsolable, Hero threw herself into the sea to join him.

Nef, which the Jason camp takes, in its literal form, as 'ship', is actually an abbreviation of *néfaste*, which can mean either a 'day of mourning', or an 'unlucky, unpropitious day'. There is also a clever Nostradamian sub-plot at work here, centring on jokes. Hierocles – a cryptogram of *Hieron*, twinning both him and Hero – lived in the fifth century AD, and was a renowned jokester. He was actually the first person in recorded history to produce a collection entirely dedicated to jokes – only twenty-eight, to be sure, but everyone has to start somewhere.

The joke theme is echoed again in line 4, with the word *Fesulan*, for Fescennine Verses were lampoons, originating in Fescennia in Tuscany, aimed specifically at taking the mickey out of an unsuspecting audience. Mount Olympus (Olimbos), situated on the opposite shore of the Aegean Sea to the Dardanelles (*Cannakale Bogazi*), was the traditional home of Jupiter and his pantheon of gods, renowned, it has to be said, for their jokes, japes and pranks at the expense of mere mortals. The wave that swept Leander away was one such joke, probably perpetrated by Aphrodite, jealous that one of her priestesses should jilt her and worship instead at the shrine of earthly love. A new wave is promised for 2016 in what Nostradamus seems to feel will be another mocking gesture by the gods. Does he refer to the change of leadership at the centre of world power – today's Washington in place of the Olympus of myth – that enthroned Donald Trump? The new president has referred to global climate change and its predicted consequences as 'a hoax'.

SUMMARY

A catastrophic flood is threatened. Its beginnings arise in the new leadership at the centre of world power, where previously responsible environmental policies are being dismissed as unfounded.

ECOLOGICAL DISASTERS III

Par quarante ans l'Iris n'apparoistra,

Par quarante ans tous les jours sera veu

La terre aride en siccité croistra,

Et grans deluges quand sera aperceu.

ℰ

For forty years the iris will not appear

For a further forty, it shall be seen every day

The already arid earth will grow still more parched

Great floods, when the iris is seen again.

In Old French *iris* was both a rainbow and an iris (the flower) – the first is meant metaphorically, the second literally. Iris was the goddess of the rainbow, and she is the messenger of the gods when they intend discord, the rainbow being the bridge from heaven let down for her convenience in carrying her message. The iris flower is a commonplace one, and of no special significance except in its very mundanity. Nostradamus seems to be implying that if we have reached a stage in our treatment of the planet in which such a simple organism as a flower can no longer grow, then we have reached crisis point. The last two lines are as clear a picture of global warming, followed by torrential flooding after the wholesale destruction of our moisture-holding forests, as we are ever likely to get.

In 2017, the index date for this quatrain, US President Donald Trump announced his government's withdrawal from the Paris Agreement, the most significant international treaty on the management of climate change.

SUMMARY

As the effects of climate change reach crisis point, progress towards a worldwide commitment to reverse the ecological impact is suddenly halted. Nostradamus warns that the natural life of the planet is at risk.

SCANDALS IN THE ROMAN CATHOLIC CHURCH I

DATE
2017

QUATRAIN
3 / 17

Mont Aventine brusler nuict sera veu
Le ciel bscure tout à un coup en Flandres
Quand le monarque chassera son nepveu
Leurs gens à Eglise commettront les esclandres.

ɞ

Mount Aventine will be seen burning by night

The sky will unexpectedly obscure Flanders

When the leader chases out his nephew

Church people will cause scandals.

This quatrain well illustrates the complexities of teasing meaning out of Nostradamus's words. Mount Aventine could refer to one of the Seven Hills of Rome, the Aventine. But Nostradamus, born 1503, would have known the writings of a certain Aventinus (1477–1534), also known as Johann Turmair, who originated from Absenberg, Bavaria (Latin name *Aventinum*), and was the author of a famous anti-papal treatise, Berg, which of course is German for mountain. Allowing for Nostradamus's well-known enjoyment of puns as well as the occasional eccentricities of his script, one also comes up with St Avertin, patron saint of lunatics (*avertineux* in French). *Avertineux* could also convey the meaning of a steep descent into insanity.

The total eclipse of the sun on 21 August 2017, the index date on the quatrain, was indeed visible from Flanders. At around that time, says Nostradamus, the pope will unwisely (insanely?) expel a trusted aide, creating a furore that will threaten the very foundations of the Church.

SUMMARY

A cardinal very close to the Pope departs the Vatican and causes a crisis for the Roman Catholic Church.

Editor's note: Mario Reading's 2015 interpretation of this quatrain has proved compelling. In 2017, Pope Francis gave leave to Cardinal George Pell, the third most senior official of the Catholic Church and Vatican treasurer, to travel to his native Australia, where he faced police charges of historical sexual offences.

SCANDALS IN THE ROMAN CATHOLIC CHURCH II

DATE
2017

QUATRAIN
9 / 2

Du hault du mont Aventin voix ouie,

Vuidez, vuidez de tous les deux costez,

Du sang des rouges sera l'ire assomie,

D'Arimin Prate, columna debotez.

ɤ

A voice is heard from high on Mount Aventine

Leave, leave, all of you, on both sides

Anger will only be satisfied if the reds bleed

The calumny is revealed by Rimini and Prato.

PREDICTION

Following on in meaning from the previous quatrain (3/17 - 2017), this quatrain continues the theme of a damaging schism within the Roman Catholic leadership. The pope asks the opposing sides to withdraw from the debate, but the laity demand blood (an accounting) from the cardinals. The source of the original calumny is then revealed by two Italian cardinals, born in Rimini and Prato respectively.

SUMMARY

The crisis in the Roman Catholic Church deepens, and an accounting is called for by the laity.

SCANDALS IN THE ROMAN CATHOLIC CHURCH III

DATE
2017

QUATRAIN
6 / 17

Apres les limes brusler les asiniers
Contraints seront changer habits divers
Les Saturnins bruslez par les meusniers
Hors la plupart qui ne sera convers.

೪

After their correction has burnt the ass drivers

They will be forced out of their habits and
into new clothing

The Saturnians are roasted by the millers

Though most of them will not be converted.

The index date is the giveaway here – 2017. A continuation of Nostradamus's prophecies (3/17 – 2017 and 9/2 – 2017) concerning the scandals in the Roman Catholic Church. 'Ass drivers' in line 1, is a comical euphemism for the priesthood, who will be forced to change out of their 'habits and into new clothing' – they will be defrocked, in other words. Ptolemy (Claudius Ptolemaeus), the celebrated mathematician, astronomer and geographer, said in his *Compost* (which Nostradamus would certainly have read in the normal course of his education): 'The children of the sayd *Saturne* shall be great jangeleres and chyders ... and they will never forgyve tyll they be revenged of theyr quarrel.' So despite being 'put through the mill', most of the recalcitrant priests (the *Saturnians*) will refuse to back down from their entrenched positions, and may well go so far as to found a schismatic Church to counter the established Church of Rome.

SUMMARY

Seeking to avert a catastrophe, the pope defrocks a number of prominent schismatics. There is the real danger of a fundamental rift in the Roman Catholic Church if matters are not quickly brought to order.

ISLAMIC ATTACK ON A NORTHERN FRENCH PORT

DATE
2018

QUATRAIN
1 / 18

Par la discorde negligence Gauloyse,

Sera passaige a Mahommet ouvert:

De sang trempé la terre & mer Senoyse,

Le port Phocen de voilles & nefs couvert.

ೞ

Because of French carelessness and misunderstanding

The Mohammedans will find a way in

Blood will soak the Seine by land & sea

The Phocensian port will fill with sails & vessels.

Given the index date of 18 and that the events described do not appear to coincide with any earlier years bearing that postscript, it seems reasonable to suppose that this quatrain refers to the year 2018.

Nostradamus would appear to be describing an attack by Islamic forces on the northern part of the French coast, up near the mouth of the Seine (Le Havre, Deauville, or Rouen, presumably). The mention of the 'Phocensian port' affords the beleaguered French a ray of hope, however, in that the men of Phocis were historically famous for turning defeat into victory through a final last-ditch effort (intending to immolate themselves and their families on a gigantic pyre if things didn't pan out). Having nothing left to lose, they threw themselves at the enemy and, extraordinarily, succeeded in driving them off.

SUMMARY

A prescient quatrain, detailing an Islamic attack on France facilitated by 'French carelessness'. Nostradamus suggests, however, that the French will ultimately prevail thanks to a courageous last-ditch stand against the invaders.

Editor's note: This quatrain appeared, verbatim, in the 2006 and 2010 editions of this book, with an update in the 2015 edition following the *Charlie Hebdo* attack of January in that year. As subsequent acts of Islamic terrorism in France have shown, the quatrain can clearly be seen as a prescient warning to the French against complacency and inaction.

EMMANUEL MACRON

A soubstenir la grand cappe troublee,

Pour l'esclaircir les rouges marcheront,

De mort famille sera presque accablee.

Les rouges le rouge assomeront.

༒

To uphold the great Cappel amid confusion,

The reds will march to assert their support

Of a family almost overwhelmed by death.

The reds will fell the red.

PREDICTION

Jacques Cappel was a leading French law officer and contemporary of Nostradamus. As advocate-general of France, he mediated in the wars between his king, Francis I, and Holy Roman Emperor Charles V. Cappel founded a major dynasty of jurists and theologians of whom several became renowned Protestant scholars. This was a family that sought peace, the rule of law and unity. Revered by reformers they also faced mortal danger from opponents in church and state at a time of bitter religious and political division.

Does Nostradamus foresee a future French mediator who seeks to unite a divided France? Emmanuel Macron, the political outsider elected president in 2017, faces the formidable task of rescuing the Republic from bankruptcy, corruption and disorder by way of radical reform. He will face determined and quite possibly violent resistance from an entrenched public sector, trades unions and extremist groups of both left and right. Nostradamus sees 2019, the index date of this quatrain, as the flashpoint.

The *rouges* of the quatrain are cast as supporters of enlightenment and reform, predicting the scarlet-attired idealists of the Commune of Paris in 1871, whose mission ended in a bloodbath. In 2019, one new red faction will overcome another.

SUMMARY

A courageous leader takes on vested interests in France in a bid to save the nation from ruin. The outcome is uncertain.

UK FAILS TO EXIT
THE EUROPEAN UNION

DATE
2019

QUATRAIN
4 / 2 1

Le changement sera fort difficile,

Cité, province au change gain fera

Coeur baut, prudent mis, chasse lui habile,

Mer, terre, peuple son estat changera.

ℰ

Changing will be impossibly difficult

Town and country will profit from

The action of a prudent, stout-hearted man in disguise

The people of land and sea will change their stance.

The United Kingdom fails to exit the European Union. The 'Brexit' process, triggered by the referendum of 2016, could not be completed by the treaty date of 2019. While the UK puts up no candidates for the scheduled elections to the European Parliament in that year, it does continue with EU membership on other terms, confirmed in 2021, the index date of this quatrain. An unidentified figure persuades all sides that this compromise will be to the benefit of Europe as a whole. It may even rescue the whole continent from chaos.

The people of land and sea in the European context must be the British, but the prudent, stout-hearted man is a mystery. A pan-European arbitrator, perhaps, who stays in the shadows – and possibly conceals the true terms from public knowledge – to reconcile the EU's competing interests. There are certainly plenty of possible candidates.

SUMMARY

Britain alters its plans for exiting the European Union. The remaining member nations, along with the semi-detached UK, reap real benefits from the compromise thanks to a mysterious leader.

TERRORIST ATTACK IN SOUTHERN FRANCE

Au port d'Agde trois fustes entreront
Portant d'infect non foi et pestilence
Passant le pont mil milles embleront,
Et le pont rompre à tierce resistance.

ℰ

Three low-slung ships enter the port of Agde

Carrying infected unbelievers and plagues

Many things will happen, a million souls will die

The bridge will break at the third arch.

Some juicy puns, here, with four separate meanings for *pont*, as in, the bridge of a ship, much water passing under a bridge, a traditional bridge, and a metaphorical bridge. In addition, a *ponté* is a decked boat, though not dissimilar to the *fuste* mentioned in line 1, which is a thin, flat vessel. *Pont* is also an abbreviation for the pontiff, or pope. Bridges in medieval France were traditionally built with three arches and three towers (a good example is Pont Valentré in Cahors), and *ponte* meant both the 'laying of eggs' and the 'ace of trumps'. All this to show how rich a brew even an apparently straightforward quatrain by Nostradamus can be.

However we choose to untangle the wordplay, though, one thing is clear – the Mediterranean coast of France is in for a terrorist attack by men carrying the plague (both spiritual and biochemical) inside them. The bridge mentioned in line 4 is perhaps that of *Al Serat*, the ordeal bridge over which all Mohammedans must pass on their way to the resurrection. It is only as wide as the blade of a scimitar, and the faithful may cross over in perfect safety, while sinners will topple over the edge, into hell. It would surely not be stretching a point too far to read line 4 as Nostradamus's belief that the bringing of plague on their enemies makes of every Mohammedan who supports the act a sinner, overloading *Al Serat*, and causing it to fracture at the third arch?

SUMMARY

A terrorist attack through the French port of Agde, with suicidal extremists incubating biochemical infections.

BIRTH OF AN ISLAND

Profonde argile blanche nourrit rocher,

Qui d'un abysme istra lacticineuse

En vain troublez ne le seront toucher,

Ignorant étre au fond terre argileuse.

ʊ

A deep white clay feeds the rock

Which boils up from an abyss like milk

Needlessly afraid, the people won't touch it

Being ignorant of the clay in the earth's heart.

The image of a 'rock boiling up like milk' brings to mind the spontaneous creation of the island of Surtsey, near the Vestmannaeyjar (Westman Islands), off the southern coast of Iceland, which began on 15 November 1963. This was a spectacular fire-and-brimstone birth, in which ash, pumice and cinders burst 1,000 feet into the sky, after more than six invisible months spent travelling to the ocean's surface. At times the ash column reached heights of 30,000 feet, and was visible from as far away as Reykjavik. Volcanic activity is commonplace beneath the surface of the oceans, so anticipating the location of any new arrival is difficult. But Nostradamus describes an environment here that is still relatively primitive – an environment possibly closed off to Western eyes. North Korea? The Indonesian Archipelago? Cuba?

SUMMARY

The birth of a new island, due to undersea volcanic activity, in an area of the world still off limits to the West.

SUCCESSION TO THE UK THRONE

Par fureur faincte d'esmotion divine,
Sera la femme du grand fort violee
Juges voulans damner telle doctrine,
Victime au peuple ignorant imolee.

ꙮ

Through the pretend fury of divine emotion

The wife of the great one will be badly wronged

Judges wish to condemn such a doctrine

The victim will be sacrificed to the ignorant people.

The future King Charles III and his Princess Consort, the former Camilla Parker Bowles, will find themselves faced with a constitutional crisis on the death of Charles's mother, Queen Elizabeth II. This crisis will be provoked by the Church of England, which is traditionally headed by the monarch. The General Synod, motivated by a desire to run its own affairs without interference from the State, will contrive the crisis based on an attack on the couple's civil wedding. Legally, the attack will be without foundation, and judgment will be found in the couple's favour, but, by using the power of the proletariat (e.g. through the media), the General Synod will get its way. The relevant index date is afforded by the next quatrain, 10/22 – 2022, which continues the prediction.

SUMMARY

A constitutional crisis occurs on the death of Queen Elizabeth II. Disestablishment of the Church of England, thanks to the civil nature of Charles's second marriage to the former Camilla Parker Bowles, is a distinct possibility.

ABDICATION OF CHARLES III OF ENGLAND

DATE
2022

QUATRAIN
10/22

Pour ne vouloir consentir à divorce,
Qui puis apres sera cogneu indigne,
Le Roi des Isles sera chassé par force
Mis à son lieu que de roi n'aura signe.

ʊ

Because they disapproved of his divorce

A man, who, later, they considered unworthy

The people will force out the King of the Islands

A man will replace him who never expected to be king.

This quatrain will come as no surprise to the British people, and it has wide implications. The preamble is that Queen Elizabeth II will die, circa 2022, at the age of around ninety-six, five years short of her mother's term of life. Prince Charles will be crowned in her stead, and become 'King of the Islands', the implication here being that he is no longer king of the other regions in the world over which his mother reigned – Canada, Australia, New Zealand, etc. – which will have, in the interim, become republics. Prince Charles will be seventy-four years old in 2022, when he takes over the throne, but the resentments held against him by a certain proportion of the British population, following his divorce from Diana, Princess of Wales, still persist. The pressure on him is so great, and his age so much against him, that Charles agrees to abdicate in favour of his elder son, Prince William.

SUMMARY

King Charles III of England, weary at the persistent attacks on both himself and his second wife in the twenty-five years since the death of his first wife, Princess Diana, decides to abdicate in favour of Prince William.

POOR SIR BEVIS

Le camp Ascap d'Europe partira,
S'adjoignant proche de l'isle submergée
D'Arton classe phalange pliera,
Nombril du monde plus grand voix subrogée.

ʊ

The Ascap camp leaves Europe

Re-forming near the submerged island

The d'Arton fleet folds and bends

A new world centre, with a louder voice, replaces it.

Commentators love this quatrain as it is so infinitely amenable and full of happy wordplays, like *Ascap* and *d'Arton*, affording seemingly endless vistas of speculative possibility, twinned with not a little innocent amusement. Most leap on the 'Nato' for *d'Arton* bandwagon, while others concentrate on the *Ascap/Ascop* Greek dimension, which gives us 'aimless' or 'imprudent'. *Camp*, too, is a juicy conundrum, and can be construed as meaning anything from an 'army', through a 'scholars' holiday', to a 'plumped-up domestic fowl'. It can also, of course, mean 'camp'.

This commentator's guess is that Nostradamus has split *Ascap* and *partira* on purpose, to disguise the identity of Ascapart, the thirty-foot giant (he had a twelve-inch gap between both eyes) who conquered Sir Bevis of Southampton and carried both him, his wife, and his horse off underneath one arm [*see* Shakespeare's *Henry VI Part Two*, act ii. 3]. Originally known as *Boeve d'Haumtone*, this well-known thirteenth-century Anglo-Norman *chanson de geste* went through many transmogrifications, *à la Don Quixote*, and was still much read in Nostradamus's time. The United Kingdom connection is further reinforced by Nostradamus's customary use of the 'submerged island' image for the British Isles, and given the index date, which closely matches that of 1/21 – 2021 [Birth of an Island], and the series of quatrains about the British royal family contained in 10/21, 6/72, and in particular, 10/22, in which the island image reoccurs, it seems foolhardy to assume that they are not, in some way, connected.

It's devilishly tempting, too, to look for a misspelling in the word *d'Arton*, giving us *Daron*, which, in Old French, was a sobriquet given to shopkeepers – for this would lead us towards the delightful image of Samuel Adams's 'nation of shopkeepers' (i.e. the British) taking to the sea in a decidedly leaky boat. If readers feel that the Samuel Adams connection is a remotely tenable one, then the final line leads us neatly back to the United States, in the temporary guise of the monster Ascapart, taking over from Britain as the dominant world power. Where this leaves poor Sir Bevis of Southampton, though, is anybody's guess.

SUMMARY

Nostradamus casts his eye over the new great imperial power, the United States, and compares it with the old imperial power it eventually took over from, Great Britain. His comparison is not complimentary to the United States.

SUBJECT

NEW FIRST FAMILY – PRECURSOR

DATE
2023

QUATRAIN
5/23

Les deux contens seront unis ensemble

Quand la pluspart à Mars seront conjoinct

Le grand d'Affrique en effrayeur et tremble

Duumvirat par la classe desjoinct.

The two contenders will unite together

When most others unite with Mars

The African leader is fearful, and trembles

The dual alliance is separated by the fleet.

This seems to be a precursor to 6/24 – 2024 [New First Family], not only in its use of the word *conjoint* but also in its concentration on dualism (*Duumvirat*) and its emphasis on the link with Mars. It seems that a false alliance is undertaken, although both sides, curiously, have made the connection in good faith. Quatrain 6/24 has the alliance as that between a strong man and a weak one, or even a male and a female leader. That said, the alliance does not, in fact, break up, but out of havoc brings appeasement – an appeasement which is, by its very nature, only a temporary alleviation of a fundamental problem.

SUMMARY

Two great powers unite in order to combat a global increase in internecine warfare. The alliance is a curious one, and works almost despite itself. Its good effects will not be long lasting, however.

NEW FIRST FAMILY

Mars et le sceptre se trouvera conjoinct,

Dessoubz Cancer calamiteuse guerre

Un peu apres sera nouveau Roi oingt,

Qui par long temps pacifiera la terre.

ᴝ

Mars and the sceptre are like husband and wife

Under Cancer there will be a calamitous war

Soon afterwards a new King will be anointed

Who, for a long time, will appease the earth.

Nothing is quite as it seems in this quatrain. *Conjoint* does not simply mean joined, as most commentators would have it, but in Old French, it implies a husband and wife, or an established common-law couple. Now here, all of a sudden, we find warlike Mars married to the virginal Sceptre, symbol of sovereignty and control, and most probably a reference to Agamemnon's famous sceptre, originally forged by Vulcan, and revered for its capacity to produce miracles.

Cancer, the crab, is famous for having bitten Hercules on the foot during his battle with the Hydra – before it had time to scuttle away, however, it was squished by the mighty one. Juno (who had sent the hapless crustacean after Hercules in the first place) took pity on the crumpled beast, and dispatched it to heaven, where it was made one of the twelve signs of the zodiac. So are Mars, Hercules, Agamemnon's Sceptre, and Cancer some kind of hidden code? This commentator's guess is that the Mars-like Agamemnon is the key, a man who sacrificed his own daughter Iphigenia to appease the goddess Diana and guarantee fair winds for the Greek fleet on their way to Troy. Clytemnestra, Agamemnon's adulterous wife, later slew him in his bath, and was killed, in her turn, by their son Orestes. Just your normal, everyday First Family.

The alliance between the two great powers, mentioned in the last quatrain, will continue. One will sacrifice the other, leaving only one leader to appease the world.

SUNNI/SHIITE WAR

Le prince Arabe Mars, Sol, Venus, Lyon

Regne d'Eglise par mer succombera

Devers la Perse bien pres d'un million

Bisance, Egypte, ver. serp. invadera.

ॐ

The Arab prince Mars, the Sun, Venus and the Lion

The reign of the Church will be vanquished at sea

Close to a million men will head towards Persia,

Byzantium, Egypt, the followers of the true
serpent will invade.

This is a complex quatrain to untangle, and it would seem wiser, for reasons that one trusts will become obvious, to start at the end. The phrase 'followers of the true serpent' defines any class, dogma or religion that seeks to undermine Christianity – in this case Nostradamus would appear to be talking of the Arabs (ergo Muslims). Christian iconography persistently translates the serpent into either Satan, or the Tempter, and he is usually pictured crushed underfoot by St Cecilia, St Euphemia, or, thanks to the promise made to Eve after the Fall ['And I will put enmity between thee and the woman, and between thy seed and her seed; it shall bruise thy head, and thou shalt bruise his heel.' Gen. iii. 15.], he finds himself placed beneath the feet of the Virgin.

Now we go back to line 1, and the Arab prince and his attributes. Mars, as we know, is the alchemical symbol for iron, the Sun for gold, and Venus for copper [*see* 4/28 – 2028: Discovery of the Philosopher's Stone], and all of these metals are presumably transmuted, as we see from line 1, into human characteristics. The Lion, as ultimate benefactor of these transmutations, is the traditional agnomen accorded to a succession of great Arab leaders, amongst whom we find Ali, cousin and son-in-law of Muhammad, whose mother called him Al Haòdara, or the Rugged Lion, at his birth; Alp Abslan, the son of Togrul Beg, the Perso-Turkish monarch who was known as the Valiant Lion; Ali Pasha, who was known as the Lion of Janina before his overthrow by Ibrahim Pasha in 1822; and Hamza, Muhammad's uncle, known as the 'Lion of God and of His Prophet' after his arrival in heaven. So it seems, at first glance, that we are dealing here with a religious war, or lesser jihad. But the million-strong army mentioned in line 3 is heading *towards*, and not away from, Arab lands. Could we then be talking of a Sunni/Shiite rift?

The Sunnis, who constitute the majority of the Muslim world, have traditionally regarded Shiism as verging on the heretical, while the Shiites, who make up approximately ten per cent of Muslims, see themselves as representing the purist strand of Islam. Nostradamus, from both his Catholic and Jewish perspectives, would of course view both strands of Islam as equally snaky.

SUMMARY

The rift between Sunni and Shiite deepens, leading to war.

SIX LUCKY GAMBLERS

Dedans les isles de cinq fleuves à un,

Par le croissant du grand Chyren Selin

Par les bruines de l'aer fureur de l'un,

Six eschapés, cachés fardeaux de lin.

༒

In the islands where five rivers flow into one

By the crescent of the great Chyren Selin

The fury of one man will float on the mist

Six will escape, hidden in a load of linen.

The 'great Chyren Selin' has appeared, in one guise or another, in eleven other Nostradamian quatrains, and he presents us with something of a problem. The crescent mentioned here gives us a clue, though, and points to an Islamic connection, as the Sultan Othman, founder of the great Turkish Empire (Ottoman), allegedly had a vision of a crescent moon spreading its horns from east to west, and later took it as his standard – the crescent still appears on the Turkish flag to this day. The moon connection is heightened by the word *Selin*, for Selene was the fecund moon goddess who rode through the heavens on a chariot drawn by two white horses, and had more than fifty daughters.

Chyren is often taken as a cryptogram for Henry, but he may more sensibly be equated with Charon (pronounced Chyren), the boatman of the River Styx, who required payment, in the form of a penny, to ferry dead souls across to Hades. Charon was also the personification of the darkness of the earth, which brings us back, once again, to the crescent moon, which throws but little light.

All that said, we are left with 'the islands where five rivers flow into one'. This may be taken not only geographically, but also metaphorically, as five, or the *pentad*, is the great mystic number, and represents the unity of God alone (without creation). The fact that 'six will escape' also has significance, as the number six means everything or nothing, and referred, in Greek and Roman times, to the random throw of three dice.

In our painfully literal modern-day world, it might be tempting to discount all the previous clues, and simply take the quatrain as it stands. That would be a mistake. If five is the great mystic number, and it flows into one (God), then Chyren Selin is the ferryman, embodiment of the darkness that awaits us before the resurrection – for Hades was not hell, of course, but rather an antechamber to either Erebus (the darkness before the light of Paradise) or Tartarus (that part of the infernal regions where the wicked are punished). The 'six that escape, hidden in a load of linen', refers back to the habit of burying the dead in a linen shroud, and one might be tempted to infer that these six escapees were gambling men, who tricked the furious Charon out of his coin (and the customary one-hundred-year penalty for those who did not pay his toll), and snuck in beneath the wire, just like Alexandre Dumas's Count of Monte Cristo did, during his escape from the Château d'If.

SUMMARY

Punjab, in Hindi, means 'five rivers', and it is conceivable that Nostradamus is speaking of a war between India and Pakistan, as the region of the Punjab is divided between the two countries. The quatrain remains a resolutely personal one, though, and more than a little opaque.

DISCOVERY OF THE PHILOSOPHER'S STONE

Lors que Venus du Sol sera couvert,

Soubs l'esplendeur sera forme occulte

Mercure au feu les aura descouvert,

Par bruit bellique sera mis à l'insulte.

༄

When Venus is covered by the sun

Shapes will be concealed beneath its splendour

Mercury, with its fire, will expose them

They will be misused in war.

In Olympiodorus's *Meteorologica*, Venus was associated with copper, the sun with gold, and the planet Mercury (Hermes) with mercury. All are alchemical totems. We are dealing, therefore, with the transmutation of metals (mercury into gold, say), a theory devised by the ancient Greeks and elaborated by the Arab and Latin alchemists who followed them. This was a search for the *prima materia* (prime matter, or the soul of mercury), and we know, from Nostradamus's mention of philosophical mercury and its 'fire' (which was thought to consist of sulphur, or its hybrid, the Philosopher's Stone), that he believes it will be discovered around this date.

This seems strange, as Nostradamus must have read Paracelsus during his medical studies (which he completed in 1529, a bare three years after Paracelsus had achieved his widest fame), and been aware of Paracelsus's opinion that the true object of alchemy was not the making of gold, but rather the preparation of medicines and the clarification of the homeopathic principle. Be that as it may, Nostradamus declares here that the Philosopher's Stone will definitely be discovered, and that it will subsequently be misused in warfare. Given the advanced state of chemical science in the twenty-first century, who dares gainsay him?

SUMMARY

Nostradamus is probably describing the first use of cloned human beings in conventional warfare.

THE SUN I

L'Oriental sortira de son siege,

Passer les monts Apennins voir la Gaule

Transpercera le ciel les eaux et neige,

Et un chacun frappera de sa gaule.

♃

The man from the East will leave his home

And cross the Apennine Mountains, to see France

He will pierce through the skies, the seas, and the snow

He will strike everyone with his staff.

The sun rises in the east (at least we hope so), and people are buried with their feet towards the east to show that they died in the hope of resurrection. We turn to the east when saying the Creed, and even the Greeks insisted that their cadavers should lie face upwards, and with their feet pointed towards Elysium – well away from the inferno in the west, in other words, and the sinister regions of the night. The east, then, is a powerful concept, and the place towards which we customarily look for enlightenment. All this to say that Nostradamus was most probably alluding to the sun, when he spoke of the 'man from the east', and if one reads the quatrain in that way, it is actually rather beautiful.

Another reading would judge the 'enlightenment' from the east metaphorically, as spiritual enlightenment. Here the concept of the 'staff' comes in, with its evocations of the ancient sceptre, which traditionally meant power, authority and dignity. Kings, of course, struck chosen recipients with their staff to raise them high in the realm, and to 'strike one's staff' also meant to lodge somewhere for the night, with the staff, in this instance, implying a tent-staff. This brings us neatly back to the sun, and to its role in creating a suitable environment in which to grow bread – a.k.a. the 'staff of life'. So perhaps this is a prayer?

The return to spiritual values foreseen in the last quatrain is reinforced in this hymn to the abundance of the sun, and to enlightenment.

THE SUN II

2029

4 / 2 9

Le Sol caché eclipse par Mercure,
Ne sera mis que pour le ciel second
De Vulcan Hermes sera faicte pasture,
Sol sera veu pur, rutilant et blond.

♏

The sun is hidden, eclipsed by Mercury

It will take second place in the sky

Hermes will be eaten by Vulcan

The sun will be seen, pure, gleaming and fair.

PREDICTION

This time we are dealing not with a prayer but with an invocation. An invocation to change. The image of Mercury is the key, with its evocations of alchemy and the transformation of base metals – we know, of course, that tiny Mercury (which is about the same size as the earth, and is the nearest planet to the sun) would not be capable of eclipsing the sun *except* in metaphor. So the sun is temporarily eclipsed by the power of mankind.

However, Hermes (the Greek Mercury, and in this case the symbol of the onward thrust of mankind's scientific discovery) proves to have been, quite literally, playing with fire, for he finds himself eaten, in his turn, by Vulcan, the blacksmith, whose dominion fire is (as it was of Hephaestus, with whom he is often identified). The sun, in the guise of Apollo, the great moral champion, is not so easily cowed by human actions, though, and soon shows Hephaestus who is the real boss of fire, as Milton describes in *Paradise Lost*, Book 1, from line 742 onwards:

> Sheer o'er the crystal battlements: from morn
> To noon he fell, from noon to dewy eve,
> A summer's day, and with the setting sun
> Dropt from the zenith, like a falling star.

So this is a warning, then, after the elucidatory prayer of thanks in the previous quatrain – a warning not to tinker with things greater than ourselves, and which we don't fully understand [*see* 4/28 – 2028: Discovery of the Philosopher's Stone]. Icarus, son of the talented but elusive Daedalus (himself a descendant of Hephaestus), thought that he, too, could challenge the sun, and look what happened to him. The wax on his man-made wings melted, and he fell into the Aegean Sea, part of which, as a sop, was named in his memory.

SUMMARY

Nostradamus warns of the seductive dangers of science to morality and right-thinking. This quatrain is a paean to philosophy.

THE SUN IS BLOTTED OUT & SECRETS LOST

2030

4/30

Plus xi. fois Luna. Sol. [orig. in ideogram]
ne voudra,

Tous augmentés & baissés de degré:

Et si bas mis que peu or lon coudra:

Qu'apres faim, perte descouvert le secret.

ꙮ

More than eleven times the moon will not want the sun

Each augmenting and declining by degree

Placed so low that little gold will be seen whilst sewing

So that, after famine, the discovery of the secret
will be lost.

PREDICTION

Nostradamus appears to be suggesting here that the natural cycles of the planets will be broken, and that the sun will fail to light the world, causing famine. His pun on the word *or* in line 3 (*or* can mean both 'gold', in the sense of the sunrise and of alchemy, and 'now') also suggests a link to the secret of the philosopher's stone [*see* 1/42 – 1642: The Search for the Philosopher's Stone and 4/28 – 2028: Discovery of the Philosopher's Stone]. If the philosopher's stone is discovered, as Nostradamus elsewhere suggests, in 2028, then the date of this quatrain may be set at 2030, when the newly found secret is once again lost [*see* 2/29 and 4/29 – 2029: The Sun I & II].

SUMMARY

Nostradamus foretells a brief two-year hiatus in human ignorance (2028–30), during which the secrets of the philosopher's stone are briefly known. Then the sun is concealed for eleven days (a comet strike or a volcanic eruption are the possible causes), and, for whatever reason, 'the secret will be lost'.

SUBJECT
POLITICAL CORRECTNESS I

DATE
2032

QUATRAIN
4/32

Es lieux et temps chair un poisson donra lieu
La loi commune sera faicte au contraire
Vieux tiendra fort plus osté du millieu
Le Pánta chiona philòn mis fort arriere.

A time will come when meat gives way to fish

Communal law will go against the people

The old order will fight hard and then be ousted

The will of the people will be repulsed.

Meat will be banned. Vegetarianism will be enforced through the common law. Despite a valiant rearguard action by the old guard (unregenerate libertarians?) the State will succeed in imposing its will on the people. Many otherwise liberal states are already heading in this direction, with restrictions on the smoking of tobacco and on free speech, amongst other things. The picture Nostradamus conjures up for us is far worse, however, and if his predictions prove true, George Orwell's *1984* will have come that little bit closer.

SUMMARY

A warning of the dangers of woolly thinking, and the loss of our capacity to discriminate for fear of offending others. This will lead to the downfall of democracy under the false guise of inclusion.

BIRTH OF THE THIRD ANTICHRIST – PRESAGE I

2032

7 / 32

Du mont Royal naistra d'une casane,

Qui cave, et compte viendra tyranniser

Dresser copie de la marche Millane,

Favene, Florence d'or et gens espuiser.

Though born in poverty, he will take supreme power

He will tyrannize and bankrupt his people

Raising a thousand-year army

Though lucky, he costs lives and gold.

This is a presage to the great quatrain number 3/35 – 2035 [Birth of the Third Antichrist]. Nostradamus often plays these games, referring back to earlier quatrains whose meaning he was unsure of at the time. There is much wordplay in this one, which would allow for two separate readings. However, if we acknowledge the wordplay, and do not take *Millane*, *Favene* and *Florence* as literally meaning 'Milan', 'Faenza' and 'Florence', we come up with *mille ans* for *Millane* ('a thousand years'), *sa veine* ('his luck') for *Favene*, and 'gold florins' for *Florence d'or*. Place names were rarely fixed in Nostradamus, and were often capitalized to draw attention to themselves and to the secrets hidden inside them, as with his use of the word *Hister*, for example, in the famous Hitler quatrains presaging the Second World War (Hitler was most probably the second Antichrist). *Hister* can also mean the Danube, near which Hitler was born, and also hysteria, from which Hitler undoubtedly suffered. The source of the word comes from the ancient Greek, *hustéra*, meaning womb, thus reinforcing the concept of a birth.

The third Antichrist will soon be born. His birth will be a disaster for the world.

BIRTH OF THE THIRD ANTICHRIST – PRESAGE II

2032

2 / 3 2

Laict, sang grenouilles escoudre en Dalmatie
Conflict donné, peste pres de Balennes
Cri sera grand par toute Esclavonie
Lors naistra monstre pres et dedans Ravenne.

ʕ

Milk and the blood of frogs flows in Dalmatia

Battle is joined, there is plague near Balennes

Wailing will echo throughout enslaved Slovenia

When the monster is born in and near Ravenna.

The second of three presages to quatrain number 3/35 – 2035 [Birth of the Third Antichrist] contains a rather nice reference to one of Aesop's fables. A frog and a mouse decide to engage in single combat to settle the question of who owns the marsh they both live in. With the battle well under way, and their attention concentrated elsewhere, an artful kite swoops down unexpectedly and carries both combatants off. Ancient Dalmatia lies almost entirely inside modern-day Croatia, which has traditionally been fought over by the Serbs and the Croats [see 9/60 – 2060: Serbo-Croatian Conflict] – it hardly stretches the imagination, therefore, to imagine the Serbs as frogs and the Croats as mice, and the Muslim minority, or perhaps even the Russians, as the artful kite? Either way, battle is joined near *Balennes* (which is probably Baleni Romini, in Romania, situated forty miles north of Bucharest).

The monster, or third Antichrist, is then born in, or near, Ravenna. It may, at this point, be apposite to explain that as well as the more obvious Ravenna, in Italy, there are also two Ravennas in the country formerly known as Yugoslavia. One, Ravna Reka, is in Serbia, and the other, Ravne na Koroskem, is in Slovenia, which ties in quite nicely with line 3.

SUMMARY

The three possible sites of the third Antichrist's birth are given. Bad luck will come to those countries abutting the place.

US PRESIDENTIAL ELECTION

Le grand empire chacun an devoir estre

Un sur les autres le viendra obtenir

Mais peu de temps sera son regne et estre

Deux ans aux naves se pourra soustenir.

ʊ

The great empire will continue, year on year

One man will snatch it from the others

Both his life and his reign will be brief

He will only carry the load for two years.

This is a non-specific quatrain about duty, and about *estre*, or 'being' (the 's' having been replaced by a circumflex in modern French), with the key word, *naves*, occurring in line 4. *Navée* means 'a large load', and the man who snatches control of the empire – which in this case can only mean the United States, the last great empire left on earth – finds the burden a heavy one, and will remain in office for only half a term as president. Whether this means that he is impeached, or dies, is not made entirely clear, although line 3 appears to direct us towards the latter.

SUMMARY

A US president finds the weight of high office too much for him, and succumbs under the strain. He manages to complete only half his term.

CLASS WAR

Par Fraude regne, forces expolier,
La classe obsesse, passages à l'espie
Deux fainctz amis se viendront rallier,
Esveiller haine de long temps assoupie.

༄

Trickery will reign, the army will be stripped

An obsession with class, spying given free rein

False friends will unite

Hatred, once quiescent, will be reawakened.

Following on in date from 4/32 – 2032 [Political Correctness I], this quatrain describes a time in which class divisions are rekindled, in which Big Brother is watching us with a less than fraternal attention, and in which the army – the sometime final protection against State tyranny – is stripped of its powers through fraud and trickery. Alliances will be contrived, not to say expedient, and will be driven, not by a sense of political duty, but by hate. Individuals will be encouraged to spy on each other, to denounce their neighbour, and even to conduct witch hunts, just as happened in the notoriously illiberal period running up to and during the Second World War, in Spain under General Franco, in Germany under Adolf Hitler, in Russia under Joseph Stalin, and in France under Maréchal Pétain. All these regimes were obsessed with class, and purported to be governing on behalf of the so-called proletariat while in fact they were busy promulgating their very own forms of plutocracy.

SUMMARY

Class warfare will be rekindled under the guise of social inclusion. The army will be fatally weakened. Politicians will wield too much power. A reaction will set in.

POLITICAL CORRECTNESS II

En grand regret sera la gent Gauloise

Coeur vain, legier croirera temerité

Pain, sel, ne vin, eaue: venin ne cervoise

Plus grand aptive, faim, froit, necessité.

೮

The French nation will be consumed by regret

With a frivolous heart, they trusted to rashness

Bread, salt, no wine, water; poison, not beer

Their leader made captive: hunger, cold, and want ensue.

Moving directly on from 4/32 – 2032 [Political Correctness I], and from 7/33 – 2033 [Class War], this quatrain continues the theme of enforced vegetarianism and alcoholic prohibition in a country previously renowned for its progressive tolerance of all the diverse strands of human behaviour – i.e. France. Wine and beer are banned, and meat, once the staple of an enlightened French cuisine, has given way to fish (as we know from 4/32). The leader of the old guard, who obviously fights a valiant rearguard action against the illiberal restrictions, is imprisoned. Catastrophe ensues.

SUMMARY

The historical lessons about prohibiting others from doing what they enjoy have not been learned. Politicians, wielding greater than usual power, abuse it. People, deprived of their pleasures, and lacking joy, lose heart.

POLITICAL CORRECTNESS III

L'ire insensee du combat furieux

Fera à table par freres le fer luire

Les despartir, blessée, curieux

Le fier duelle viendra en France nuire.

༄

The senseless anger of the furious war

Will cause brothers to unsheathe their knives
across the table

Driven apart, wounded, prying

The pride-driven duel will hurt France.

Civil unrest has now come to France, as a result of the increasingly demented strictures of the European superstate [see 7/34 – 2034: Political Correctness II]. The French people, never ones to allow themselves to be controlled by laws they despise, are forced into a virtual civil war, where brother fights brother 'across the table'. The 'across the table' image also contains within itself a sneaking reference to the banning of meat and game, for which, in peasant France, the near-ubiquitous knife would be used, in, amongst other things, the bleeding of rabbits [see 4/32 – 2032: Political Correctness I].

'Prying', in line 3, is a direct reference to 'spying' in line 2 of 7/33 – 2033 [Class War], and to the rekindling by the State of a situation last encountered during the Second World War under the Pétainiste government of unoccupied Vichy France, when informing on one's neighbour was positively encouraged.

SUMMARY

The French finally rebel against the evils of political correctness and spoilsport politics. The great traditions of the barricade, and the proletarian fight for freedom, are reawakened.

BIRTH OF THE THIRD ANTICHRIST – PRESAGE III

Quand le deffaut du Soleil lors sera.
Sur le plain jour le monstre sera veu
Tout autrement on l'interpretera,
Cherté n'a garde mil n'y aura pourveu.

At the total eclipse of the sun

The monster will be seen in broad daylight

He will be misinterpreted

None will have foreseen the great cost.

In 2034 a total eclipse of the sun is expected on 20 March, a little ahead of the sun's transit from Pisces into Aries, the sign of wars, famines, heat, droughts, and magical transformation. The eclipse will pass over central Africa, the Middle East (including Egypt and Iran), and south Asia (including India and China). It will presage the birth of the third Antichrist [3/35 – 2035], and he will be conceived in the period immediately following the eclipse, and born in the new year. We know that this is a significant presage because of the paradox hidden within the quatrain, namely that 'at the total eclipse of the sun' (i.e. when all is darkness), 'the monster will be seen in *broad daylight*'. We also know from 2/32 – 2032 that the monster (from the Latin *monstrum* meaning not only a prodigy, or monster, but also an omen, or scourge) will be born in Italy, Serbia or Slovenia, all areas well outside the line of the eclipse. His coming will be welcomed by many with secret vested interests, but it will ultimately portend disaster.

SUMMARY

The third Antichrist is conceived, in darkness, during the total eclipse. He will be born into darkness, too, and he will bring darkness upon the world.

WINTER FREEZE

Dedans l'entrée de Garonne et Baise

Et la forest non loing de Damazan

Du Marsaves gelees, puis gresle et bize

Dordonnois gelle par erreur de Mezan.

At the entrance to the Garonne and Bazas

And the forest close to Damazan

Mont-de-Marsan is frozen, then hail and northerly winds

Dordogne freezes, but in the wrong house (Mézin).

The geographical location of this great frost is absolutely specific, and earlier commentators appear to have missed that *Baise* is Bazan, *Mezan* is Mézin, and *Marsaves* is the Mont-de-Marsan. All the places mentioned are located within a forty-mile radius of each other, on the south bank of the River Garonne, in south-western France, and Nostradamus, as usual, is enjoying his puns, with *Mezan* and *maison* (house) neatly juxtaposed. The Dordogne (situated sixty miles to the north) is renowned for its abominable winter weather, with temperatures of as low as -15°C not uncommon, and Nostradamus implies here that, in this particular winter of 2035, the usual freeze will happen in the wrong place.

SUMMARY

A terrible winter freeze will hit the towns and villages on the south bank of the Garonne. The people will not be expecting it. It will catch them catastrophically unprepared.

BIRTH OF THE THIRD ANTICHRIST

Du plus profond de l'Occident d'Europe
De pauvres gens un jeune enfant naistra
Qui par sa langue seduira grande troupe,
Son bruit au regne d'Orient plus croistra.

From deep in the western part of Europe

A child will be born, to poor parents

He will seduce the multitude with his tongue

The noise of his reputation will grow in the eastern kingdom.

This new leader of the Muslim world will be around thirty-five years old by the time of the global war referred to in quatrain number 5/70 - 2070. Though only from a humble background in the western Islamic diaspora, he will manage to pull together the equivalent of the old Ottoman Empire by the seductive power of his language, and threaten the dominant positions of the US and China. This will result in a catastrophic nuclear war, 'powerful enough to disturb mountains' [*see* 5/70]. The worrying aspect of this quatrain lies in the word *seduira*, 'to seduce' or 'deceive by charm', in line 3, with its implication that this leader will be a manipulator and a fixer, and also in the word *bruit* in line 4, implying that his reputation will be spun as a form of narrative, rather than fairly earned. It's a worrying quatrain in every respect, and echoes the presage of Adolf Hitler, as the possible second Antichrist, in the now famous quatrain 2/24:

> *Bestes farouches de faim fleuves tranner,*
> *Plus part du champ encontre Hister sera.*
> *En caige de fer le grand fera treisner,*
> *Quand rien enfant de Germain observera.*

> With the hunger of wild beasts they cross rivers
> Most of the world will be against Hister
> The great man will find himself inside a cage
>   of iron
> The German child understands nothing.

This is the closest Nostradamus ever came to a warning to the future world, and the subtle language he uses in 3/35 - 2035 echoes this, with its hints of hidden depths and secret manipulations.

SUMMARY

The third Antichrist is born. The die has been cast. The future of the world, unless a miracle occurs, will be very bleak, with global warfare and ecological damage on an unprecedented scale.

BIRTH OF THE THIRD ANTICHRIST – CONSEQUENCES

2036

9/36

Un grand Roi prins entre les mains d'un Joine,

Non loing de Pasque confusion coup coultre

Perpet. captifs temps que fouldre en la husne,

Lorsque trois freres se blesseront et meutre.

༄

A great King falls into the hands of a youngster

There is confusion around Easter time,
and a knife-blow

Long-term captives, and St Elmo's Fire

When three brothers wound and kill each other.

This is not the only time that Nostradamus uses the image of St Elmo's Fire [*see* 2/90 – 2090: Hungary in Crisis]. He has also used the concept of 'three brothers' before, particularly in 8/46 – 2005 [Death of Pope John Paul II]. In that quatrain the 'three brothers' symbolized the Magi, and, given the Easter motif in this quatrain, there is no reason to suppose that he is not using the same trope once again. One's instinct is to connect this quatrain with that of the preceding year, 3/35 – 2035 [Birth of the Third Antichrist], and if that is the case, Nostradamus is giving us a second warning. The 'child born to poor parents' is most definitely *not* the Second Coming, as, in his case, the Magi (figuratively) fall out. The mention of 'Easter time' is an obvious reference to the death of Christ, and this is further strengthened by the mention of a 'knife-blow', which equates with the lance driven into Jesus' side. Given all this, it would appear that the 'great King' in line 1 refers directly to Jesus, and that it is he, or more correctly his followers, who risk falling into the hands of 'the youngster', causing confusion.

SUMMARY

The third Antichrist will be declared the Second Coming. This will not be true. He will damage both the world and the Christian Church.

WAR BETWEEN AUSTRALIA & INDONESIA

DATE

EARLY 2037

QUATRAIN

1 / 37

Un peu devant que le soleil s'excuse,

Conflict donné grand peuple dubiteux

Profliges, port marin ne faict response,

Pont et sepulchre en deux estranges lieux.

ʊ

Shortly before the eclipse of the sun

A war is triggered by a great nation of unbelievers

Wastefully, the seaport does not fight back

Bridge and memorial are dissevered.

The total solar eclipse of 13 July 2037 virtually splits Australia in two, from north to south, exiting between Sydney and Brisbane to finish up over the South Island of New Zealand. Australia is the 'great nation of unbelievers' (secular state), therefore, and the war Nostradamus predicts is started by them.

When we turn to the three clues Nostradamus gives us about the nation it attacks, 'the seaport', 'the bridge', and 'the memorial', we find ourselves inexorably drawn towards Surabaya, the second largest city and seaport in Indonesia after Jakarta, and home to more than three million people. Surabaya's largest monument, Tugu Pahlawan, is a memorial to the heroes who died during Indonesia's struggle for independence from 1945 to 1949, and the famous Red Bridge (Jembatan Merah), now known as China Town, is the site of the Great Battle of Surabaya, which took place on 10 November 1945.

SUMMARY

Indonesia and Australia fall out over supremacy in the Indian Ocean. The dispute snowballs into armed conflict, followed by all-out war.

GRECO-TURKISH
PROBLEM

DATE

2039

QUATRAIN

4 / 39

Les Rhodians demanderont secours
Par le neglect de ses hors delaissée
L'Empire Arabe revalera son secours
Par Hesperies la cause redressée.

℧

The people of Rhodes will ask for help

Robbed, thanks to the actions of their forebears

The Arab Empire returns like for like

Its cause is straightened out by the West.

PREDICTION

The island of Rhodes lies about as near to the Turkish mainland as one can get without actually becoming a part of it, and even a cursory glance at a map of the Aegean area will afford one an unsettling insight into some of the causes of the ancient antagonism between Turkey and Greece. It's all too intimate by half down there, and the powder keg looks set to blow again. A fair partition, in Turkish terms, would give them Rhodes, Kos, Samos, Lesbos and Khios, etc., and probably Ikaria too. Assuming, for a moment, that Turkey is now in the EU, some accommodation may one day have to be made, just as it has been made on Cyprus [*see* 3/89 - 2089: Cyprus Partition]. Given the increasing dependence on Arab oil by the Western economies, enlightened pragmatism may well be the name of the game here.

SUMMARY

The ancient antagonism between the Greeks and the Turks over national boundaries reignites. The rift is so great that independent arbitration is called for.

GREAT STORM

Un peus apres non point longue intervalle
Par mer et terre sera faict grand tumulte
Beaucoup plus grande sera pugne navalle,
Feux, animaux, qui feront plus d'insulte.

༄

A short while after a previous occurrence

A further fierce storm will rise over land and sea

The sea-borne cost of this one will be even larger

Fire, animals, it will be an even greater outrage.

A double whammy. One storm hidden by another. Already reeling from the depredations of one great storm, the world will not be prepared for a second, even greater one. For a description of the effects of such a storm, one has only to go back to Nostradamus's Tsunami I prediction, in 1/29 – 2004, or forward to his future Tsunami predictions in 4/80 – 2080 and 5/81 – 2081.

SUMMARY

Just as the world is recovering from one great storm, another, worse storm follows. Communities are taken by surprise. Existing damage is compounded.

END OF MONARCHY
IN BRITAIN I

DATE
2040

QUATRAIN
10/40

Le jeune nay au regne Britannique,

Qu'aura le pere mourant recommandé,

Icelui mort Lonole donra topique,

Et à son fils le regne demandé.

༗

The young man, born to rule Britain

Though commended by his dying father

Once the father is dead, London will cavil

And the kingdom will be taken back from his son.

Following on from 6/72 - 2022 [Succession to the UK Throne] and 10/22 - 2022 [Abdication of Charles III of England], this is a particularly difficult quatrain to call. King William would be around fifty-eight years old by this date, and would have reigned for close on eighteen years. Prince George of Cambridge, heir to the throne, would be only twenty-seven in 2040, thus 'the young man, born to rule England' mentioned in line 1. Nostradamus, though, makes it clear that, despite the dying King William commending his son to the nation, following the age-old tradition, as their new monarch – London, or in this case, the will of the people, won't have it. One is forced to assume, therefore, that Nostradamus is predicting the end of the British monarchy.

SUMMARY

Some 1,210 years after King Egbert was first pronounced *Bretwalda* (Ruler of the British), the United Kingdom finally loses her monarchy.

END OF MONARCHY
IN BRITAIN II

DATE
2040

QUATRAIN
4/40

Les fortresses des assiegés serrés
Par poudre à feu profondés en abisme
Les proditeurs seront tous vifs serrés
Onc aux sacristes n'advint si piteux scisme.

༷

The castles of the besieged will be locked

They will fall because of gunpowder

The traitors will be imprisoned alive

Never before have the Saxons been so piteously divided.

This is a certain follow-on to 10/40 – 2040 [End of Monarchy in Britain I]. We know this because Nostradamus scatters a series of clues throughout the quatrain. Firstly the castles traditionally associated with the royal family – Windsor, Buckingham Palace, Balmoral, etc. – will be annexed and locked up. Secondly, the royal house will fall because of 'gunpowder' [*see* line 2], echoing the famous Gunpowder Plot of 5 November 1605 against James I, originated by Robert Catesby, and in which Guy Fawkes – later to join Joan of Arc as one of the two most famous bonfire victims in history – volunteered to set off the gunpowder.

As a monarchist himself, Nostradamus did not approve of plots against either kings or the established State, and his image, in line 3, of the traitors carrying their own imprisonment (guilt) within them, confirms that position. Line 4 is self-evident, the implication being that the British have made a grievous mistake in ridding themselves of the monarchy that has traditionally held them together as a nation, and that divisions will increase, rather than diminish, as a result.

SUMMARY

Nostradamus predicts that with the fall of its monarchy Britain will lose the cement that bound it together as a nation.

END OF MONARCHY
IN BRITAIN III

DATE
2040

QUATRAIN
5 / 40

Le sang royal sera si tresmeslé,

Contrainct seront Gaulois de l'Hesperie

On attendra que terme soit coulé,

Et que memoire de la voix soit perie.

ʊ

Royal blood will be diluted

France will be gagged by the Americans

Some time will need to pass

Until the memory of all that was said passes away.

The third of this trio of quatrains, all dealing with the British royal family and republicanism, and all categorically linked by their index dates [*see* 10/40 and 4/40 – 2040]. Hesperus (Venus) is the evening star, and is the first to appear in the western skies after the setting of the sun. The Greeks called Italy Hesperia, because to them it seemed the westernmost land. The Romans, needless to say, gave the name to Spain. For us, of course, the westernmost lands are the Americas.

Venus (Hesperus) was also the goddess of love and courtship, and there is an obvious link here with line 1, in which royal blood is seen to be diluted. Could there have been a birth out of wedlock, throwing the British succession into disarray? This might tie in with France needing to be 'gagged by the Americans', because, according to the European Constitution, a bastard child would need to be seen to have exactly the same rights as a child born inside a regularized marriage, something that does not tie in with British royal protocols. The schism between Britain and France is obviously a deep one, if the Americans are required to come in and act as referees.

SUMMARY

Republican France rejoices at the end of the British monarchy. Republican America is less triumphal, and attempts to rein France in.

BIRTH OF A VISIONARY
PAN-AFRICAN LEADER

DATE
2041

QUATRAIN
5 / 41

Nay souz les umbres et journée nocturne
Sera en rege et bonté souveraine
Fera renaistre son sang de l'antique urne,
Renouvellant siecle d'or pour l'aerain.

༡

Born inside the shadows, on the very day of an eclipse

He will be sovereign in rule and goodness

He will renew his blood at the ancient urn

Restoring the golden age with bronze.

After the traumas suffered by the British royal family in 10/40, 4/40 and 5/40 – 2040, it would be nice to be able to report that a child was born to them who would rekindle a renewed respect for the monarchy. However the total eclipse Nostradamus mentions in line 1 covers Angola, the Congo, Uganda, Kenya and Somalia, and not western Europe, so it is of a Pan-African leader that we are talking here. This reading is further strengthened by the expression 'ancient urn' in line 3, for we now know that Africa, and in particular the geographical areas comprised within Kenya and Tanzania, was, in all probability, the cradle of human life.

'Bronze', too, has its role to play in this reading, as it was one of the earliest known alloys, and is cast on a bed of clay. The strong implication in line 4, then, is that we need to revert to the simplicities and certainties of the past in order to be able to renew the future, and that the great African leader Nostradamus speaks of will achieve this miracle.

This is a deeply optimistic quatrain, and very comforting in the light of the horrors awaiting humanity in the next fifty years. Perhaps Africa, wisely led for a change, will be able to hold itself apart from the world conflict, and present itself as an agent for renewal at a time of global upheaval?

SUMMARY

A great African leader is born. He will unite traditionally disparate tribes and countries, affording Africa, for only the second time in its post-colonial history, a significant influence for good on the world stage.

RELIGIOUS WARS I

Seront ouys au ceil les armes battre

Celuy an mesme les divins ennemis,

Voudront Loix Sainctes injustement debatre,

Par foudre et guerre bien croyants a mort mis.

༽

Weapons of war will scream in the sky

That same year even holy men will become enemies

They will unfairly attempt to suppress the Sacred Law

True believers will die by war and shock.

The 'Sacred Law' is probably the Ten Commandments, which in Nostradamus's time was also a euphemism for the scratching of the face with ten fingers, in the case of a woman, or the smashing action of two male fists, in that of a man. Shakespeare was conversant with the concept too, and used the image in *Henry VI Part Two*, act i. 3: 'Could I come near your beauty with my nails, I'd set my ten commandments in your face.' Sir Walter Scott uses a similar metaphor in *Waverley*, so it was not simply a Shakespearean trope. It could, however, also be applied to the Sharia, or Sacred Law of Islam, the amalgam of four otherwise disparate schools of Sunni thought comprising the Koran, the *sunna*, the *ijma*, and the *qiyas*.

The term 'true believer' also tends towards the Islamic definition. Shiites, who form a minority of approximately ten per cent within the Islamic world, believe in their own set of 'sacred laws', handed down by infallible *imams*, lineal descendants from the Prophet Mohammed's cousin and son-in-law, fourth caliph Ali ibn Abi Taleb. Their traditional stronghold is in the Islamic Republic of Iran, with smaller, minority outposts in Iraq and Lebanon. When all this is taken into account, there is the strong possibility that, in 2043, we could be facing another Iran/Iraq war. The last one, which lasted from 1980 to 1988, resulted in more than a million casualties.

SUMMARY

A new Iran/Iraq war is in the offing, placing Shia against Sunni. There will be many casualties.

RELIGIOUS WARS II

Durant l'estoille chevelue apparente,
Les trois grans princes seront faits enemis
Frappés du ciel paix terre tremulante,
Pau, Timbre undans, serpent sus le bort mis.

ↄ

When the shooting star appears

The three great princes will fall out

World peace will falter, struck from the sky

Both Tiber and Po will overflow, and a serpent
will be placed on their banks.

There will be two great meteor outbursts from long-period comet dust trails during 2043 – the first will occur on 31 March, at 21.36 GMT, and the second on 22 November at 10.58 GMT. Following on from the Religious Wars of 4/43 – 2043, the three great world leaders of Russia, China and the United States will fall out over the correct way to respond to the crisis. 'Serpents', although traditionally understood to represent Satan (in Hindu mythology, hell is called Narac, the region of serpents), were also considered symbols of renovation and regeneration, and it was long assumed that they were capable, when old, of growing young again, by sloughing their timeworn skin between two rocks. Rivers, also, were seen as regenerative, and this allows us to read the last line in the quatrain as fundamentally optimistic, at least in the short term.

SUMMARY
World powers fall out over the correct way to respond to the Iran/Iraq war. The schism, though deep, is eventually papered over. The patching will be temporary.

CHEMICAL WARFARE

De nuict par Nantes l'Iris apparoistra,

Des artz marins susciteront la pluie

Arabique goulfre grand classe parfondra,

Un monstre en Saxe naistra d'ours et truie.

ℰ

A rainbow will appear, by night, near Nantes

Seafaring men will call up artificial rain

A great fleet will be fused in the Arabian gulf

In Saxony, a monster will be born of a bear and a sow.

This quatrain must be approached metaphorically, as much as literally. First we have Iris, in line 1, goddess of the rainbow, but also the messenger of the gods when they intend to sow discord. Why Nantes? Perhaps because it is a major port, and a manufacturing centre of chemicals, which would tie in with the creation of seeded, or 'artificial', rain. The word *parfondre* is a tricky one, and no longer used in modern French. In Old French it means to fuse, or melt together, and was much used in alchemy, and in the making of enamel. In this context it could mean both melted, in its literal sense, and destroyed, in its metaphorical sense, as mechanical objects that are fused together can no longer, by definition, function.

Saxony is an ancient region in north-western Europe, upon which Charlemagne imposed Christianity in 772 AD – it is now part of a reunified Germany. The 'bear' almost always refers to Russia, but it also means 'independence', as in Dryden's 'The Hind and the Panther':

> *The bloody bear, an independent beast,*
> *Unlicked to form, in groans her hate expressed.*

The concept of the 'sow' meant that someone had got hold of the wrong vessel (a sow was a tub with handles), as in 'You have got hold of the wrong sow by the ear' – the 'bear' and the 'sow' are also inimical, one being independent and free, the other being domesticated. Given all this, it would seem that the quatrain foretells a time when chemical warfare is again on the agenda, and that Nostradamus feels that this is very wrong. A 'monster' is born by the fusing of disparate elements that were never meant to be united, and this will sow discord, as exemplified by the appearance of the goddess Iris over the French factory that manufactures these articles.

SUMMARY

Great strides are made, in secret, in the realm of chemical warfare. Nostradamus warns that the genie must not be let out of the bottle.

CATHOLIC/JEWISH MISCEGENATION

Trop le ciel pleure l'Androgyn procrée,
Pres de ciel sang humain respondu
Par mort trop tard grand peuple recrée,
Tard et tost vient le secours attendu.

How heaven mourns the birth of the Hermaphrodite

Near to heaven, human blood is shed

Too late, through death, a great people are recreated

Help comes both too early, and too late

The 'monster, born of a bear and a sow' mentioned in 6/44 – 2044 [Chemical Warfare], is echoed here, a year later, in the birth of the 'hermaphrodite'. Hermaphroditus was the son of Hermes and Aphrodite. He was so beautiful that the nymph Salmacis (whose name was later given to a fountain in Caria which turned all those who bathed in it effeminate), fell passionately in love with him, and prayed to the gods that they might become one. The gods, with their rather robust sense of humour, took her at her word, and the two became united in one body.

Ancient French law, in a rather uncharacteristic fit of tolerance, acknowledged the existence of hermaphrodites, and allowed them considerable latitude, and the Jews too, through the Talmud, gave them special privileges – such forbearance, though, probably refers back to Genesis i. 27 and Genesis ii. 20–24, and to God's creation of woman from Adam's rib, rather than to any more enlightened motivation. In other cultures, in particular that of ancient Athens, hermaphrodites were put to death as unnatural, while the Hindus and the Chinese insisted that the hermaphrodite choose one sex, and then stick to it willy-nilly.

Given the context, it is at least possible that Nostradamus is mourning an 'unnatural' mating of two sexes into one, possibly as a result of human interference – if this is indeed the case, then a reference back to the Chemical Warfare discussed in 6/44 – 2044 is the most likely source of the 'bear/sow' miscegenation. But perhaps he is talking of his own fusing of Catholic and Jew? In that case the 'recreation of a great people, through death' that he mentions in line 3, might refer specifically to the Jews, and Nostradamus might be foreseeing (a long shot, this, but feasible) the creation of the State of Israel on the back of the Holocaust? If that is the case, then an index date of 1945, rather than 2045 would be more apposite, allowing a three-year leeway between the true revelation of the extent of the Holocaust in 1945, and the foundation of the State of Israel (*Medinat Yisra'el*) in 1948.

SUMMARY

A warning that unnatural mixtures, either chemical or human, rarely work.

COLLECTIVE UNCONSCIOUS

DATE
2046

QUATRAIN
2 / 46

Apres grand troche humaine plus grand s'appreste,

Le grand moteur des Siecles renouvelle

Pluie, sang, laict, famine, fer et peste,

Au ciel veu feu, courant long estincelle.

᭬

Following one great human tragedy, a greater
lies in wait

The mighty movement of the centuries
brings renewal

Rain, blood, milk, famine, sword and the plague

Fire will be seen in the sky, with a trail of sparks.

PREDICTION

In its renewal theme, this quatrain harks back to 2/43 – 2043 [Religious Wars II], but the renewal in question seems Dionysiac, rather than Apollonian (*pace* Nietzsche's *Birth of Tragedy*) – violent and visceral, that is, rather than gradual and germane. Yet another link to 2/43 comes in the 'shooting star' image, and one sometimes wonders whether, in a sort of spontaneous morphology, the accrued wisdom of past ages isn't transmitted down the centuries in the form of unconscious remembrance, as promulgated in Jung's concept of the collective unconscious, or even the Akashic records. This would explain, too, why humanity persists in viewing the arrival of comets, meteors, asteroids, and shooting stars, etc., as harbingers of change, or precursors of apocalyptic events. If we have a collective unconscious memory of past strikes and their aftermaths, then it is hardly surprising that, when faced with the possibility of an extraterrestrial impact, we anticipate, and even promulgate, dynamic change.

SUMMARY

There will be a restlessness throughout the earth as people prepare, intuitively, for the coming of a great catastrophe. Signs will be sought, and auguries looked for.

METEOR STRIKES AS HARBINGERS OF CHANGE

DATE
2046

QUATRAIN
1 / 46

Tout aupres d'Auch, de Lectoure et Mirande,

Grande feu du ciel en trois nuits tombera,

Chose adviendra bien stupende et mirande,

Bien peu après al terre tremblera.

In the vicinity of Auch, Lectoure and Mirande

A great fire will fall from the sky for three nights

A stupendous, well-aimed, and spectacular occurrence

Soon afterwards the earth will tremble and be ruffled.

Once again we find that quatrain index dates are linked in meaning across different Nostradamian *Centuries*. This time 1/46 shares the image of a 'great fire falling from the sky' with its near twin, 2/46 – 2046 [Collective Unconscious], which gives us 'fire will be seen in the sky'. This quatrain, too, uses pun and wordplay to deflect our attention from a more literal reading of the text. To *mire* in Old French, is to aim a gun, and *al terre* in line 4 contains the double meaning of 'all the world' and to be 'ruffled', or 'irritated'.

Nostradamus would have known the towns of Auch, Lectoure and Mirande very well from his period of residence in Agen, in the Gers. It was there, of course, that he lost his first wife and their two children to the plague, so the place would have had mixed memories for him, of both past happiness and present grief. All the more reason then to look beyond the literal to a spiritual renewal, brought about by a physical cataclysm. For Nostradamus, the physical cataclysm would have been the death of his family, the trauma of which helped to trigger his prophetic powers. For the earth to change, and to discover its own hidden resources, Nostradamus anticipates the need for a greater – dare one say even communal – cataclysm.

SUMMARY

Some see global catastrophe as the essential trigger needed for fundamental spiritual change, while others fear the onslaught of uncertainty.

MAFIA KILLING I

Lac Trasmenien portera tesmoignage
Des conjurez serez dedans Perouse
Un despolle contrefera le sage
Truant Tedesque de sterne et minuse.

༄

Lake Trasimeno will show

That the conspirators are to be found in Perugia

A despot will imitate a sage

Killing the German through the breastbone and face.

A secret is discovered in Lake Trasimeno (situated only a few miles from Perugia), which throws light on a murder committed previously, on a German. *Des conjurez* means 'those who have sworn an oath', and we know that, in Italy, the Cosa Nostra requires such a blood oath from all its members. Founded in the thirteenth century as a secret society, the Mafia remains a powerful force in southern Italian society to this day, so Nostradamus's inspired 'a despot will imitate a sage' image probably applies to a publicity-hungry Mafia leader who grabs the high moral ground without having earned it, possibly as a result of a prominent court case.

SUMMARY

A high-profile Mafia killing garners headlines. A *Capo di Tutti Capi* (Mafia boss of bosses) makes the most of his day in court.

MAFIA KILLING II

Du Lac Lemans les sermons fasceront,
Des jours seront reduit par des sepmains,
Puis mois, puis an, puis tous dafaliront,
Les Magistrats damneront leurs loix vaines.

ঽ

Oaths will be taken on Lake Leman

Days will become weeks

Then months, then a year: all will default

Magistrates will curse their useless laws.

Curious, the use of 'lakes' in this quatrain, 1/47, and also in its twin, 8/47 – 2047 [Mafia Killing I]. Knowing what we do of Nostradamus, there is almost bound to be a connection. *Tedesque*, in line 4 of 8/47, nominally means a German (from the Old French *Tudesque*, or Teutonic), but can also mean a German speaker, or speaker of *Schwyzertütsch* (Swiss German), an Alemannic language.

The two quatrains are also joined by the concept of oaths, and the dual meaning of *sepmains*, in line 2, which can mean both a week, and the bringing together of seven hands in the forming, let's say, of a secret society (Cosa Nostra). The number 'seven', as we remember from 5/81 – 2081 [Tsunami III], is a holy number, but it can also encompass the seven deadly sins of Pride, Wrath, Envy, Lust, Gluttony, Avarice, and Sloth – all notable adjuncts of the criminal classes. The number seven is also used indefinitely, to signify a long time – Shakespeare talks of a man being 'a vile thief this seven year'. Given all this, it seems that we are presented with a mysterious death, in these two quatrains, and the inability of the authorities either to catch, or to have condemned, the miscreants who perpetrated it.

SUMMARY

Interpol are powerless in the face of the *omertà* (silence towards the authorities) promulgated by Mafia members. The murderers of the prominent German are never caught.

GLOBAL WARMING II

Plannure, Ausonne fertille, spacieuse,
Produira tabons si tant de sauterelles:
Clarté solaire deviendra nubileuse,
Ronger tout, grand peste venir d'elles.

ဗု

The scorching of the wide, fertile plains of Bordeaux

Will produce so many gadflies and locusts

That sunlight will become opaque

They will devour everything, bringing a terrible plague.

PREDICTION

The word *planure* is Old French for the burning of wood shavings, and implies a relentless, dry heat, such as is commonly found in Africa just before the onset of a locust attack. Nostradamus's description of the wide, fertile plains of Bordeaux purposefully plays up the distinction between the traditional plenty of Europe, and the relative poverty of the African savannah. Things are set to change, however, unless we are more careful in how we treat our planet. The wine harvest, symbol of European civilization since Roman times, will be decimated, and we shall have brought a plague on all our houses.

SUMMARY

Dry winds, more commonly seen in desert regions, will strike the European mainland, devastating the wine harvest.

US HURRICANES/ GLOBAL WARMING III

DATE
2048

QUATRAIN
9/48

La grand cité d'occean maritime

Environnee de maretz en cristal

Dans le solstice hyemal et la prime

Sera tempté de vent espouvantal.

ೞ

The great maritime ocean city

Surrounded by salt marshes

In both the winter solstice and the spring

Will be tormented by a frightful wind.

PREDICTION

The fallout from 4/48 – 2048 [Global Warming II] will continue all the way from the coming of spring until the winter solstice, which occurs on or around 21 December. Ocean City is situated in Worcester County, Maryland, one hundred miles from the Annapolis Naval Academy, and surrounded by the Sinepuxent and Assateague salt marshes. Norfolk, Virginia, which boasts one of the world's largest concentrations of naval installations, combining seaports, naval bases, training schools, and dockyards, is a bare one hundred miles to the south. The area is already renowned for the severity of its Atlantic gales, and the two hurricanes which hit the area in March/April and December 2048 will be real lulus, conjured up by a rapidly warming planet.

SUMMARY

An area on the US Atlantic coast will be devastated by twin hurricanes. Important naval installations will be affected.

FRENCH IMMIGRATION

Regne Gaulois tu seras bien changé

En lieu estrange est translaté l'empire

En autres moeurs et lois seras rangé

Roan, et Chartres te feront bien du pire.

ℰℐ

French State, you will be changed

Your realm will be modified in singular ways

Rouen will be eaten by other laws and customs

Chartres will be even worse.

Ever since the revolution of 1789, France has considered itself a secular state. This secularism is now challenged by the ever increasing pressure of immigrants, who claim the right to be judged, not by the laws of their adopted country, but by those of the countries and cultures they have nominally left behind. Nostradamus sees this as a threat, and indulges in the vocative case as a clear warning to his country of the threat involved. It should be remembered that Nostradamus came from a family of assimilated Jews, and it is likely that he would have felt strongly about the subject of integration for this reason. The State, in Nostradamus's view, should be more important than the individual. To that extent he was a Confucian, and the idea that immigrants should stand upon their rights and insist on being judged by different laws from those of the host country which welcomed them would have been an anathema to him.

SUMMARY

Uncontrolled immigration is starting to impact on the traditionally tolerant French way of life. Minority groups assert their right to be judged by the laws of the country of their origin, rather than by those of their host state.

TERRORISM

QUATRAIN
9 / 51

Contre les rouges sectes se banderont,

Feu, eau, fer, corde par paix se minera,

Au point mourir, ceux qui machineront,

Fors un que monde surtout ruinera.

ꙮ

They will unite against the red sects

The peace will be undermined by fire, water and iron

The plotters will die by the sword

Except one, whom the people will destroy.

PREDICTION

Red is the colour of magic. In Roman times it denoted war, and a call to arms. Even in the Royal Navy, the hoisting of a red flag indicated that no quarter would be asked for, or given. In France Since 1791, red has also been the symbol of insurrection and terrorism, of radicalism and anarchy. Nostradamus sees nations uniting against the terrorists, who use every possible method to undermine the peace. When you die by the sword, you die by your own hand. These terrorists consider themselves martyrs, and are prepared to die for their cause – all save one, whom the crowd despatch before he is able to trigger the explosives he is carrying on his person.

SUMMARY

Terrorism is on the increase, threatening the democratic stability of a number of European states. Civil populations belatedly retaliate.

EMANCIPATION OF MUSLIM WOMEN

DATE
2052

QUATRAIN
4 / 5 2

En cité obsesse aux murs hommes et femmes,

Ennemis hors le chef prest à soi rendre

Vent sera fort encontre les gendarmes,

Chassez seront par chaux, poussiere, et cendre.

༄

A city obsessed by walls between the sexes

Finds the enemy outside and its chief priest
prepared to surrender

The wind will fan the sparks

They will be driven off by heat, dust and cinders.

This is a fascinating quatrain, and not at all easy to read, given the double meanings in each line. The key, curiously enough, comes in line 3, with the word *gendarmes*. The traditional meaning would seem to be 'men-at-arms', or 'policemen' – in Old French, however, *gendarmes* can also mean 'sparks from a wood fire'. Once we realize this, it becomes clear that each line contains a single key word, with two quite separate meanings attached to it. In line 2 we have *prest*, meaning both 'priest' and 'prepared', and in line 1 *obsesse*, meaning both 'obsessed' and 'besieged'. In line 4 *chaux* can mean both 'lime' (used for breaking down dead bodies), and 'heat'. Nothing, it seems, is to be taken too literally.

A translation, with the alternative meanings in place, is given on the previous page. Its meaning is only too clear, especially when taken with 9/51 – 2051 [Terrorism]. A Muslim city, run by Taliban priests, which is both a seat of terrorism and a place where men and women are rigorously segregated, is besieged by pro-Western forces. The city is burnt, with the burning acting in a purifying capacity. One can only assume that following the city's purification (its liming), an emancipation of sorts follows.

SUMMARY

The downfall of a Muslim city and of a priestly class. This leads to a liberalization of certain religious laws dealing with the relations between men and women, and with women's place in a fundamentalist Islamic society.

BATTLE OF THE SEXES

La loi du Sol, et Venus contendens,

Appropriant l'esprit de prophetie

Ne l'un ne l'autre ne seront entendus,

Par Sol tiendra la loy du grand Messie.

ও

The laws of the sun and of Venus will clash

Appropriating the spirit of prophecy

Neither the one nor the other will be heard

The Great Messiah's law will prevail through the sun.

It is very clear, through the twinning of Apollo, god of the sun, and Venus, goddess of love, that we are dealing with a male/female equation here. As well as being the god of light, Apollo also rules over flocks and pastures and is the source of the male nomadic tradition and attraction to the wilderness, whereas Venus, goddess of gardens, epitomizes the female urge towards domestication. Apollo's laws (which are those that eventually prevail, according to Nostradamus) encourage fair play and moral excellence, while discouraging vengeance. Venus's laws encourage courtship and chastity, and are protective, rather than creative. Nostradamus appears to be describing the dangers of an over-feminization of culture, not in a pejorative way, it needs to be added, but as a stifle to creativity, perhaps in the guise of over-regulation and political correctness [*see* 4/32 – 2032 & 7/34 – 2034].

SUMMARY

Nostradamus puts the ancient male/female equation of risk versus caution under the microscope, and predicts that risk will eventually have to win the day if society is to progress in any direction other than sideways.

BOOK BURNING

QUATRAIN
9 / 53

Le Neron jeune dans les trois cheminées

Fera de paiges vifs pour ardoir getter,

Heureux qui loing sera de telz menees,

Trois de son sang le feront mort guetter.

ℰ

The young Nero, using three chimneys

Will burn the living word in his ardour

Happy the person far from such practices

Three of his own blood will watch him die.

PREDICTION

Part of a trio of quatrains [*see* also 4/52 – 2052: Emancipation of Muslim Women and 2/54 – 2054: Monsoon Rains] which deal with the restrictive practices put into place by a fundamentalist Muslim state. The number three also arises twice within the quatrain, and is thus significant. Pythagoras considered it the perfect number, expressive of a beginning, a middle and an end.

In this case we are dealing with the burning of books deemed blasphemous by the mullahs. Nero was a leader intimately associated with fire, who may or may not, as Roman Emperor, have ordered the burning of Rome. At the very least, or so it is alleged, he forbade the putting out of the fire, because he 'wanted to see how Troy would look when it was in flames'. But a 'Nero' is also a generic term for any bloody-minded man, relentless tyrant, or evildoer of extraordinary savagery. Could this young Nero be the now twenty-one-year-old man Nostradamus speaks of in 7/32 – 2032 [Birth of the Third Antichrist – Presage I]? If so the number three would exactly describe his life, and its effect, for as we know from the Bible, 'the enemies of man are threefold – the world, the flesh and the devil'.

The quatrain, too, is in three stages: the 'young' Nero, with his three chimneys; the 'mature' Nero, who burns books; and the 'dead' Nero, killed by 'three of his own blood'. There are, of course, three Antichrists, too. Napoleon/Stalin, Hitler, and the strangely persuasive gentleman whose birth is announced in 3/35 – 2035 [Birth of the Third Antichrist].

SUMMARY

This is a plea against censorship, and in favour of freedom. The third Antichrist is building his power base by playing on his followers' greed for power over others, just as Adolf Hitler manipulated his followers through the gift of favours and of political and civic office.

SUBJECT

MONSOON RAINS

DATE
2054

QUATRAIN
2/54

Par gent estrange, et Romains lointaine

Leur grand cité apres eaue fort troublée

Fille sans trop different domaine

Prins chef, ferreure n'avoir este riblée.

Foreigners, far from Rome

Their great city will be damaged by rainfall

A girl from not that far away

Is taken by their leader, her old bonds still in place.

The key to this quatrain lies in the concept of 'far from Rome', which implies a Muslim city (as far from Roman Catholicism as one can get), damaged by torrential rainfall, possibly as a result of the global warming Nostradamus predicts in 4/48 – 2048 [Global Warming II]. The capture of the girl is more obscure, and may simply be a symbolical reference to a generalized loss of freedom, particularly given the reference to 'old bonds'. Another reading, though, would have the girl representing Muslim womanhood, and the 'old bonds still in place' would then refer to the restrictions placed upon females in a traditional Islamic society, restrictions which would be redoubled following a crisis.

SUMMARY

Emergency powers are triggered by a terrible flood. These are later misused in order to control and limit the freedoms of women in a traditionalist society.

US/CHINESE
STANDOFF

Deux revoltes faicte du maling falcigere,

De regne et siecles faict permutation

Le mobil signe à son endroit si ingere,

Aux deux egaux et d'inclination.

ʊ

Two revolutions, thanks to the cunning scythe-bearer

Kingdoms will alter in the new century

Libra will move into its house

And both sides are well balanced.

The key to both the date and the meaning of this quatrain is the mobile sign of Libra – even the placing of the quatrain, as number fifty-four in Nostradamus's first cycle of one hundred, sets it at the fulcrum, or point of balance, of the century. In astrological terms, Libra comes at a time, between 22 September and 22 October, when both day and night, if weighed, would be found to be in balance. Saturn, of course, is the 'scythe-bearer' and devourer of all his children, save Jupiter (air), Neptune (water) and Pluto (the grave) – in his other guise as Kronos (time), he cannot, of course, consume *them*. Thus the two opposing sides, America and China, will find themselves equally balanced. The world will be split between day and night, and east and west, and neither side will be able to consume the other.

SUMMARY

China and the United States are now equally powerful and equally influential on the world stage. A treaty is agreed, defusing potential areas of conflict. There is a temporary standoff.

US/CHINESE FALSE DAWN

Les malheureuses nopces celebreront

En grand joye mais la fin malheureuse

Mary et mere nore desdaigneront

Le Phybe mort et nore plus piteuse.

 εϑ

They will celebrate the unfortunate wedding

With great joy, but it will have an unhappy end

Husband and mother will scorn the new bride

With Phoebus dead, the north has an even worse fate.

We know from Nostradamus's tone, and his use of the classical allusion to Phoebus, that he does not mean us to take this quatrain literally. This is a symbolical wedding, and given the content of 1/54 – 2054 [US/Chinese Standoff], it is reasonable to suppose that the 'unfortunate wedding' is that between the US and China, a thesis further strengthened by Nostradamus's pun on the word *nore* in line 4, which can mean 'daughter-in-law', 'black' or 'the north'. Phoebus, the sun god, rises in the east, of course, and sinks in the west, and the name Phoebus itself comes from the Greek word *phao*, to shine. Should the sun stop shining, therefore, the world would be plunged into darkness, which, in this case, would appear to be the darkness of war.

SUMMARY

The pact between the United States and China remains fragile. Nostradamus warns of what will happen if the pact should ever fail.

ISLAM DISTURBS THE BALANCE OF WORLD POWER I

Soubs l'opposite climat Babylonique,
Grand sera de sang effusion
Que terre et mer, air, ciel sera inique,
Sectes, faim, regnes, pestes, confusion.

ꙮ

In the reverse of a Babylonian climate

There will be much bloodshed

Land, sea, air and heaven will be iniquitous

Sects, hunger, new kingdoms, plagues and confusion follow.

A prelude to 1/56 – 2056, this is a generalized build-up to a tense situation, where the world teeters on the brink of global war, a war that we know will in fact not occur until 2070. The concept of the 'reverse of a Babylonian climate' is an interesting one, though. Babylon means 'the gate of God', but the city had already lost its position of importance well before the rise of Islam in the seventh century AD – even Alexander the Great died before he was able to make it the capital of his mighty empire. Could the word 'climate' refer to the famous Hanging Gardens, one of the seven wonders of antiquity? The gardens were in terraces, supported by pillars, soaring to heights of more than 300 feet above the ground – so the 'climate', in other words, was an artificial one. Either way, the quatrain bodes no good for anyone.

SUMMARY

A new cold war begins between the United States and China, thanks to brinkmanship by the Arab powers. For a time there is even the threat of a global war, but this recedes.

ISLAM DISTURBS THE BALANCE OF WORLD POWER II

L'horrible guerre qu'en l'occident s'apreste
L'an ensuivant viendra la pestilence,
Si fort horribles que jeune, vieux, ne beste,
Sang, feu, Mercure, Mars, Jupiter en France.

෴

The horrible war being prepared in the West

Will be followed, the next year, by a plague

So terrible in its effect that it spares not
young, old, nor animal

Blood, fire, Mercury, Mars, Jupiter in France.

More rumblings of doom, specifically linked in index date to 1/55 – 2055 and 1/56 – 2056, and, by a longer tail, to 5/70 – 2070 [Global War I]. The 'plague' in line 2 is the great famine, delineated in 3/71 – 2071 [Global War V], which causes the United Kingdom to batten down its hatches and become Fortress Britain once again. In Camoëns's *Lusiad*, Bacchus, the evil demon, is the guardian power of Islam, and Mars (the personification of divine fortitude) is the guardian power of Christianity.

The link between Jupiter, Mercury and Paris is a more difficult one to run to ground, but for a long time there were two famous statues of Mercury in Paris, one by Lerambert, in the garden of Versailles, and another by Mellana in the Tuileries – and the sixth wonder of the ancient world was undoubtedly the statue of Olympian Jove (Jupiter) by Phidias, which was destroyed by 'fire' in Constantinople in 475 AD. In alchemical terms, fire is sulphur, while the three planets represent mercury, iron and tin, respectively. France is traditionally represented by a ship.

SUMMARY

The danger of war flares up again, but is forgotten following a worldwide epidemic, which spares no one.

ISLAM DISTURBS THE BALANCE OF WORLD POWER III

Vous verrez tost et tard taire grand change,

Horreurs extremes, et vindications

Que si la lune conduicte par son ange,

Le ciel s'approche des inclinations.

You will see, sooner or later, great changes occurring

Extreme horrors and vengeances

As if the moon, led by its angel

Approaches heaven and its inclinations.

PREDICTION

The angel Gabriel, in Jewish mythology, is the Angel of Death. In Islam, he is the Angel of Truth, the one who took Muhammad to heaven on Al-borak (the lightning), and revealed to him the prophetic lore. The 'moon', in this case, refers specifically to the crescent moon, symbol of Islam, which Muhammad, according to the Koran, cleaved in two to prove his mission to Habib the Wise. Referring back to 1/54 – 2054 [US/Chinese Standoff], we now find the Islamic world splitting the balance of world power in two, with China on the one side, and the US on the other, just as Muhammad split the moon – the implication being that the Islamic world will turn one nation state against the other for its own ends.

SUMMARY

A very dangerous game of brinkmanship is going on, with the West on one side, and China on the other, with the Islamic world providing the unstable fulcrum.

CRISIS IN THE ROMAN CATHOLIC CHURCH I

Que peste et glaive n'a sceu definer

Mort dans le puis sommet du ciel frappé

L'abbé mourra quand verra ruiner

Ceux du naufrage l'esceuil voulant grapper.

ʊ

What plague and the sword could not finish

Dies at the wellhead, struck from the sky

The abbot will die when he sees the ruin

Of those lost overboard, trying, in vain, to reclimb the ladders.

The *abbé*, in line 3, is the key to this quatrain, and refers to the pope, who will metaphorically die (lose power) thanks to the schisms in his Church. The first line harks back to the past history of the Church, and to the plagues and wars it has survived over the centuries. The second line, however, shows that the crisis, this time, will come from within – from the very Articles of Faith that underpin the Church's teachings; its 'wellhead', in other words. Once the Church loses direction, and the sense of those Articles is lost, the pope is powerless to staunch the effect this loss of faith is having on his congregation.

Line 4 is a powerful one, and portrays the Catholic Church as a ship without a crew, and possibly without a captain. The 'ladder' image is a reference to Jacob's ladder, which the patriarch saw in a vision (Genesis xxviii, 12), rising from the earth to heaven, and on which angels were perpetually ascending and descending.

SUMMARY

The pope dies, and the Catholic Church is thrown into disarray, with schisms and sects abounding. The Church seems to have lost its way.

CRISIS IN THE ROMAN CATHOLIC CHURCH II

DATE
2056

QUATRAIN
5 / 56

Par le trespas du tres vieillart pontif,
Sera esleu Romain de bon aage
Qu'il sera dict que la siege debisse,
Et long tiendra et de picquant ouvrage.

On the death of the very old pope

A Roman, in the prime of life, will succeed him

It will be said that he weakens the pontificate

That he will last long, and cause acute damage.

A direct follow-on, both in index date and meaning, from 2/56 – 2056. The old pope is dead. An Italian pope, born in Rome itself, and much younger than his predecessor, is elected in his stead. His gainsayers despair because of the possible length of his tenure as pope, and of the damage such a perceived modernizer might wreak on dogmatic tradition. They have no need to worry, however. He will be dead within a year [see 2/57 – 2057: Crisis in the Roman Catholic Church V].

SUMMARY

A much younger pope is elected, but many have misgivings as to his abilities. There is considerable resistance to his papacy.

CRISIS IN THE ROMAN CATHOLIC CHURCH III

Apres victoire de babieuse langue

L'esprit tempte en tranquil et repos

Victeur sanguin par conflict faict harangue,

Roustir la langue et la chair et les os.

છ૭

After the victory of the prattling tongues

The spirit quietens in tranquillity and repose

The victor, flushed with triumph, makes speeches

Roasted be his tongue, his flesh and his bones.

PREDICTION

A direct continuation of 2/56 & 5/56 – 2056 [Crisis in the Roman Catholic Church I & II]. The wrong man, it seems, has won. He has made his way to the vacated papacy, thanks to slander and gossip. Even at the very moment of his triumph, he cannot resist lecturing his enemies. Nostradamus wishes him consigned to hell, where the devil (presumably) will give him a warm, and possibly even infernal, welcome.

SUMMARY

The new young pope tries to cement his power base too early, and alienates more people than he pleases. The cardinals are beginning to think that they may have made a grave error in electing him.

CRISIS IN THE ROMAN CATHOLIC CHURCH IV

Le soublevé ne cognoistra son sceptre
Les enfants jeunes des plus grands honnira
Oncques ne fut un plus ord cruel estre
Pour leurs espouses mort noir bannira.

༎

The raised one will not recognize his own sceptre

The children of the great ones are disgraced

Never was there a fouler, crueller being

The black one will banish their dead spouses.

Nostradamus is having another go at the upstart pope [*see* 4/56 – 2056: Crisis in the Roman Catholic Church III]. Almost comically, he sees the new pope as having been raised from such a low position to such a high one that he is unable even to recognize the implications and responsibilities of his own rule (*sceptre*). The faithful are disgraced, and even nuns, married to Jesus Christ, find their position in the Church undermined.

SUMMARY

Thanks to premature efforts at modernization and reform, the new pope has alienated the middle ground. The climate is not right for such extreme measures.

CRISIS IN THE ROMAN CATHOLIC CHURCH V

Avant conflict le grand mur tombera
Le grand à mort, mort, trop subite et plainte
Nay imparfaict: la plus part nagera
Aupres du fleuve de sang la terre tainte.

ʊ

Before the battle can be joined, the great wall falls

The mighty one is dead, dead, before his time, complaining

Born imperfect: most will now swim

Near the river the ground is the colour of blood.

The new pope dies, only a year after his enthronement. The rift in the Catholic Church is healed. Nostradamus, who consigned this upstart pope to hell in 4/56 – 2056, must be pleased. Now those who could not 'reclimb the ladders' in 2/56 – 2056, are able to swim again. The reference to 'ground the colour of blood' refers to a meeting of the College of Cardinals in the Vatican City (situated on the west bank of the River Tiber), to elect a new Holy Father, and one, this time, who unites, rather than divides. The image is a striking one, and it is almost possible to imagine Nostradamus soaring above the russet convocation on a crane, *à la* Orson Welles, movie camera in hand.

SUMMARY

Extraordinarily, perhaps even sinisterly, the new pope dies. His death, however, provides the last chance to save the reputation and the following of a Catholic Church in crisis.

BUDDHISM &
THE PROTESTANT
CHURCH

Deux assiegez en ardente ferveur,
De soif estaincts pour deux plaines tasses
Le fort lime, et un vieillart resveur,
Au Genevois de Nira monstra trasse.

༽༽

Two will be besieged with burning fervour

Two full cups will not quench their thirst

The strong are finished, and an old dreamer

Will show the Genevans the way to Nira.

Nira, in line 4, could be either an anagram for Iran, or, taken as *n'ira*, it could mean 'not to go'. It could also be an abbreviation of the Buddhist word *nirvana*, meaning annihilation. *Nir*, in Sanskrit, means 'out', and the Gautama taught that the only way out from the accumulated pain we inherit each time we are reborn, is through *nirvana*.

Nostradamus also mentions the word 'two' on two separate occasions in the quatrain, and we know, from past experience, that this will have significance in the final reading. 'Two' was held to be the evil principle by Pythagoras, and, in consequence, the second day of the second month of the year was considered sacred to Pluto, and was unlucky, for Pluto symbolized the grave, and was the god of the dead regions. The *Genevans*, in Nostradamian code, almost invariably means the Protestants, and stems from the Geneva Doctrines of 1541, in which Calvin put forward his five great points of Calvinism.

Let's sum up the quatrain, then, given all this information: on the second day of February 2059, there will be a crisis in the Protestant Church. An elderly spiritual guide will point adherents of the old Church towards Buddhist teachings, equating the fourth point of Calvinist doctrine, namely 'particular redemption', to the fourth sublime verity of the Gautama, which is the path to the cessation of suffering.

SUMMARY

The Protestant Church has lost its direction and sense of spirituality in an ever more materialistic world. Lessons need to be learned from the wise. A teacher will appear.

ENGLAND SECEDES FROM EUROPEAN UNION

Premier en Gaule, premier en Romanie

Par mer et terre aux Anglois et Paris

Merveilleux faitz par celle grand mesnie

Violent terax perdra le Norlaris.

First in France, and now in Romania

By sea and land to the English and Paris

Marvellous deeds by that great alliance

The violent attack will lose the northern larch.

The quatrain opens with a characteristically to-the-point picture of the European Union ('the great alliance'), showing its early beginnings in France, then moving, towards England, and, later in its history (1 January 2007), even as far as Romania. Much thought has been given, during the past few centuries of Nostradamus scholarship, to the possible meanings of the word *Norlaris*, which appears in the last line of the quatrain. Most commentators agree that it must be a cryptogram for Lorraine. The answer is, in fact, much simpler than that, and relies on a simple split of the word into *Nor* (north) and *Larix* (larch). Tarver's indispensable 1849 *French Phraseological Dictionary* gives *larix* as the Latinate alternative to the French word *mélèze*, a larch tree. Nostradamus is therefore implying that the northern part of the European tree (the United Kingdom) is lost, following a violent attack from the outside.

The word *terrasser* or *terax* means to throw a man to the floor, or 'cut him down'. This reading is further strengthened by Nostradamus's wordplay on the conjunction of the words *Nor* and *Laris* – for the Lares were minor Roman deities, associated not only with the guardianship of the hearth and of the crossroads, but also (and here Nostradamus excels himself) of the State, in the form of the *Lares Praestites*.

SUMMARY

England finally withdraws from the European Union, completing the process tentatively begun 44 years previously [see 4/21 – 2019 UK Fails to exit European Union]. Scotland, Wales and Northern Ireland remain members.

SERBO-CROATIAN CONFLICT

DATE
2060

QUATRAIN
9/60

Conflict barbare, en la cornere noire,
Sang espandu trembler la Dalmatie,
Grand Ismael mettra son promontoire
Rangs trembler secours Lusitanie.

ↄↄ

A Barbary conflict in the black gutter

Blood will be spilt, rocking Dalmatia

Great Ishmael will create inroads

In the trembling ranks of the Portuguese rescuers.

Ishmael was the eldest son of the patriarch Abraham, by his Egyptian handmaiden, Hagar. When Abraham's formerly barren wife Sarah produced a son, Isaac, she contrived that Abraham send Hagar and Ishmael away, where he became the progenitor of twelve tribes of desert nomads, and the eventual patriarch of the Shiite Muslims. The mention of Barbary, in line 1, also ties in with Ishmael, as the Barbary Coast covered much of the area (modern-day Algeria, Tunisia and Libya) in which the nomadic tribes of Ishmael dwelt.

Ancient Dalmatia lies almost entirely within what we now know as Croatia, scene of the bloody conflict between Serb and Croat that lasted from 1991 to 1995, and that had both a racial and a religious basis, the Serbs being principally Eastern Orthodox, and the Croats Roman Catholic – both communities have significant Muslim minorities, however. The 'black gutter' in line 1 may be taken to point, therefore, to problems arising between the two races, triggered by the Muslim minority. The 'Portuguese rescuers' are most probably United Nations troops, sent in, yet again, as peacekeepers, and this takes on added significance when one bears in mind the previous quatrain 8/60 – 2060 [England Secedes from European Union], as the area concerned became part of the European Union in the first decade of the twenty-first century.

SUMMARY

A new Serbo-Croatian conflict will occur, necessitating the intervention of United Nations peacekeepers.

FRENCH LEADERSHIP

Le vieux mocqué et privé de sa place,

Par l'estrangier qui le subornera

Mains de son filz mangées devant sa face,

Le frere à Chartres, Orl. Rouan trahyra.

ꙫ

The old man is mocked and unseated

By the same foreigner who bribed him

He will see the hands of his son eaten in front of him

He will betray his brother at Chartres, at Orleans
and at Rouen.

In ancient Egypt hands were a symbol of fortitude, and in Rome they were a sign of fidelity. For a Roman to lay claim to a slave, he had to formally place his hands upon him in front of the *praetor* (chief law officer). Hands were a symbol of power over others, therefore, and for a father to see the hands of his son 'eaten' in front of him, was tantamount to seeing that son made powerless.

Chartres, Orleans and Rouen are all cathedral cities in France, intimately connected with the laying on of power, in the form of the laying on of a crown to a future king – the implication being that, once the son has power stripped away from him thanks to his father's corruption, his brother, too, suffers at the old man's hands. In this context, 'son' and 'brother' need not be taken literally, but may be used to imply a favoured follower, or someone being groomed for leadership.

SUMMARY

The president of France is betrayed by someone he thought was a trusted adviser. Even his anointed heir is tarnished by the scandal, and loses his position in the government.

ARAB WAR

La grand band et secte crucigere
Se dressera en Mesopotamie
Du proche fleuve compagnie legiere
Que telle loi tiendra pour ennemie.

ෆ

The great army of the people of the cross

Will draw up in Mesopotamia

A smaller company, from a nearby river

Will find their rule inimical.

The earliest communities of what the Greeks knew as Mesopotamia (the land between the rivers Tigris and Euphrates) date back to 7000 BC. The area covers the eastern part of Syria, south-eastern Turkey, and most of modern-day Iraq. The 'people of the cross' in line 1 must be taken to apply to Christians, even though we now know that the cross was also a pre-Christian emblem – Nostradamus would have been unlikely to acknowledge this fact, however.

SUMMARY

A Western army invades Arab territory. They are not made welcome, and war follows.

WORLDWIDE
EPIDEMIC

DATE
2062

QUATRAIN
2 / 6 2

Mabus puis tost alors mourra, viendra,
De gens et bestes une horrible defaite
Puis tout à coup la vengeance on verra,
Cent, main, soif, faim, quand courra la comete.

Mabus, though dead, returns

Both man and beast suffer terribly

Then, all of a sudden, vengeance arrives

Much blood, thirst, hunger, when the comet passes.

Mabus is one of the cryptograms most beloved of Nostradamus's commentators. It has been transliterated into just about everything, ranging, in ascending order of lunacy, from Saddam Hussein (via Da Vinci-esque mirror writing), to 'self-abuse', the Magus, Megabyzus, Aenobarbus, Thurbo Majus, Abu Nidal, Abu Abbas, and even as far as poor old Raymond Mabus, former Governor of Mississippi and US Ambassador to Saudi Arabia (1994–96), who found himself, through mere hazard of a name, in imminent danger of being tarred as either the third Antichrist, or, worse still, one of his victims, thanks to the efforts of a decidedly mixed bag of Nostradamian conspiracy nuts. To be fair, though, no one commentator claims to have the definitive answer, and many of these suggestions are put forward with tongue firmly in cheek.

In point of fact, Nostradamus's coining of the name Mabus probably stems from something as commonplace as his knowledge of his close contemporary, the Flemish painter Jan Gossaert (1470–1532), who was known as Mabuse after his birthplace of Maubeuge, in France (situated close to Mons, and to the borders of modern-day Belgium).

There may be a connection, too, with the legend of Queen Mab, the fairies' midwife of dreams, the title of queen referring, not to a regal background, but to the simple fact that she was a woman (equating with the still current Scots word *queynie*, and the no longer current Saxon word *quen*). So could Mabus simply mean the 'time of dreams'? If that is the case, then the quatrain takes on a haunting, doomed quality, part nightmare and part hallucination.

Whatever meaning we construe from it, 2062 sounds like a particularly bad time to be alive.

SUMMARY
An epidemic that was thought to be defeated flares up again, killing many more people than before.

PEACE REIGNS OVER THE EARTH

DATE
2063

QUATRAIN
1 / 63

Les fléaux passés diminue le monde,

Long temps la paix terres inhabitées

Seur marchera par ciel, serre, mer et onde:

Puis de nouveau les guerres suscitées.

With the plague over, the earth shrinks

Peace will reign for a good while

People will travel through the sky, like birds,
and by sea and wave

Before war once again is called for.

Following the terrible epidemic described in 2/62 – 2062 [Worldwide Epidemic], which has decimated the world population, things will return to normal for a while. There will be peace. Travel will recommence. The word *serre* in line 3 is of particular interest here, because in Old French it means the 'talon of a bird', giving an image of people travelling through the air as if carried by a hawk – one trusts it's not invidious to remind readers, at this point, that there was no such concept as 'air travel' in Nostradamus's time. Here, he is simply taking it for granted, as if his visions had vouchsafed him a sight of the future which he accepted completely, as if it were an everyday matter.

The war in line 4, of course, is the global war due in 2070 [*see* 5/70], and which he warns us about, yet again, in 10/69 – 2069. It is interesting to note that in both this quatrain and in 10/69 Nostradamus uses the word *seur*, meaning *sueur*, 'by the sweat of one's brow'. The juxtaposition of that word with *serre*, the talon of a bird, is undoubtedly intentional, and implies human, rather than divine, will, in our mastering of the elements.

SUMMARY

The earth's population has drastically shrunk, thanks to the worldwide epidemic of 2062. There is a period of calm and harmony in the world, possibly as a result of collective shock.

CONSEQUENCES OF ENGLAND'S SECESSION FROM EU

2064

8 / 64

Dedans les isles les enfans transportez,

Les deux de sept seront en desespoir,

Ceux du terrouer en seront supportez

Nom pelle prins des ligues fui l'espoir.

℃℘

Children will be moved around the islands

Two out of every seven will be in despair

The land will feed those who live by it

Only the spade will unify and give hope.

Over-populated England, deprived of EU support [*see* 8/60 – 2060: England Secedes from European Union], will be faced with a food crisis. Children will be removed from the towns and sent into what remains of the countryside. Nearly thirty per cent of the population will face starvation. Thanks to successive government policies of building houses over what remains of the green belt, not much of the English countryside survives – but those who live there, and, more importantly, those who live from it, will still thrive.

And now a short extra note on the word *pelle*, in line 4, which may provide a little insight into the method behind Nostradamus's apparent madness. To a literate French person reading this quatrain in the sixteenth or seventeenth century, the word would have a number of connotations. The obvious one would be a 'spade'. In addition there would be the concept of the 'clerk of the pells', an officer of the exchequer whose duty was to make entries on the pells, or parchment rolls. Finally, the classically trained reader would not fail to grasp a possible reference to the 'Pellean Conqueror', Alexander the Great, who was born at Pella, in Macedonia, an interpretation that would reinforce, in line 4, the need for a strong leader to save the country from crisis.

SUMMARY

England, protected in part by its geographical location from the full effects of the 2062 epidemic, finds itself faced with a food crisis. A return to the countryside is ordered, but people have become so urbanized that they no longer know how to till and harvest the land.

TREATY OF ROME

2065

10/65

O vaste Romone ta ruine s'approche,

Non de tes murs de ton sang et substance;

L'aspre par lettres fera si horrible coche,

Fer poinctu mis à tous jusques au manche.

ᘐ

O great Roman one, your ruin approaches

Not by your walls, but by your blood and substance

The asper, through letters, will cause such a
terrible rift

Pointed steel will damage everything as far as the English
Channel.

Following England's secession from the European Union [8/60 – 2060], and the EU crisis foretold in 8/64 – 2064, Nostradamus concentrates, once again, on the Treaty of Rome [see also 6/68 – 2068: Nuclear Market in Europe]. Here he shows how the main part of the 1957 treaty, which deals with the formation of the European Community, is undermined by trivial arguments about money – the asper or *aspre*, was a tiny Turkish coin worth only about the 120th part of piaster [see also 2/90 – 2090: Hungary in Crisis]. The 1957 treaty was, of course, the 'blood and substance' of the 1958 founding of the European Community, and the 'pointed steel' mentioned in line 4 was the pen used to sign it, and also to sign the documents which would eventually undermine it. The damage will be restricted to the French side of the English Channel (*la Manche*), because of England's unilateral secession from the EU five years previously.

SUMMARY

There is a crisis in the European Union. The original Treaty of Rome is under threat. England, no longer a member of the EU, stands apart from the row.

DANGERS OF EMBRYO REPLACEMENT

9 / 6 5

Dedans le coing de Luna viendra rendre,
Ou sera prins et mis en terre étrange.
Les fruits immeurs seront à grand esclandre,
Grand vitupère à l'un grande louange.

Inside the quince he will offer himself to Luna

Where he will be taken and placed in a strange land

The unripe fruits will cause great unpleasantness

Great blame, but to one, great praise.

This is a fascinating quatrain, which no commentator has come anywhere near to translating correctly. It is so full of puns and double meanings that a literal translation would appear nonsensical. One can't help wondering if Edward Lear had not read the quatrain before he wrote 'The Owl And The Pussy-Cat':

> *They dined on mince, and slices of quince,*
> *Which they ate with a runcible spoon;*
> *And hand in hand, on the edge of the sand,*
> *They danced by the light of the moon,*
> *The moon,*
> *The moon,*
> *They danced by the light of the moon.*

Luna, otherwise known as Selene, was, strictly speaking, the full moon (the moon personified), who is in love with Endymion (the setting sun). Endymion is condemned to endless sleep and everlasting youth, and Luna comes to him, every night, upon the Latmian Hills. Their meetings are fruitful, and result in fifty daughters, but Luna is fickle, and has another few daughters with Zeus, one of whom, Erse, is the dew.

Pliny mentions that the fruit of the quince was considered to ward off the evil eye, and it is represented in many Greek statues, and also on the walls of Pompeii. Nostradamus, it has to be said, was famous for his sweet tooth, and had something of a fetish for quinces, for he was the inventor of a much lauded quince jelly, which found favour in a number of great houses due to its restorative qualities – like the fig, of course, the quince is also a symbol of fertility, or fecundity, which gives the quatrain a distinctly sexual connotation. With all this in mind, and after considerable mental debate, this particular commentator will plump for a warning, by Nostradamus, about the ethical dangers of *in vitro* fertilization.

SUMMARY
A symbolic quatrain warning of the dangers of unfettered scientific tinkering, particularly in the form of fertility treatments. These have become so sophisticated, and so convenient, that they are threatening to replace nature – to our eventual cost as human beings.

ENGLAND & SCOTLAND FALL OUT OVER EU

Le chef de Londres par regne l'Americh,

L'isle de l'Escosse tempiera par gellee

Roi Reb auront un si faux antechrist

Que les mettra trestous dans la meslee.

ʊ

London's prime minister, ruled by America

Will freeze out the Scottish enclave

The Rob Roys will pick themselves so false
an Antichrist

That they will all be thrown into the mix.

This conflict stems from England's secession from the EU [8/60 – 2060] and the schism this creates with Scotland, which resolves to remain inside the community. England will align itself with its old ally, the United States, while Scotland will align itself with its 'auld ally', France.

Rob Roy, of course, was the nickname of Robert McGregor, an amiable rogue and a splendid swordsman, who assumed his mother's name of Campbell when his clan was outlawed by the Scottish Parliament of 1662 – it didn't take him very long to become Scotland's equivalent of England's Robin Hood, though, and he only evaded transportation to Barbados by a whisker. This time the Scottish 'Rob Roys' will find that the ally they have picked for themselves is full of perfidy, and leaking with ulterior motives. Is it any coincidence that the index number of this quatrain, 10/66 – 2066, also coincides with the thousand-year anniversary of the Norman Conquest?

SUMMARY

Scotland and England disagree profoundly over Scotland's membership of the European Union. England sides with the United States over matters of trade, while Scotland sides with France.

GREAT FAMINE

La grande famine que je sens approcher,
Souvent tourner, puis estre universelle
Si grand et long qu'un viendra arracher,
Du bois racine et l'enfant de mamelle.

ༀ

The great famine which I sense is approaching

Will start intermittently, but gradually
become universal

So great and so long will it be, that roots will be torn

From the trees, and infants from their
mother's breast.

Nostradamus rarely put himself forward in the first person singular, and one is forced to assume that his purpose for so doing in this quatrain is because the content distressed him in a private and personal way. During the sixteenth century, much of France was tormented by plague, famine and warfare, and Nostradamus had first-hand knowledge of this in the town in which he had chosen to make his home, and base his medical practice, Agen. When the Black Death took not only his beloved first wife, but also his two children, the townspeople turned on him, arguing that a man who could not protect his own family from the plague was hardly likely to be able to protect others. Nostradamus packed up his bags and left, but only after he had been sued for the return of his wife's dowry by her distraught family. Impecunious and heartbroken, he dedicated the rest of his medical life to eradicating the plague, becoming one of Europe's foremost authorities on the subject. So when Nostradamus conjures up an image of starving people scrabbling in desperation at the roots of trees because the harvest hasn't been gathered in, or of infants being plucked from their dead mother's breast, he knows exactly what he is talking about.

SUMMARY

Worldwide famine follows hard on the heels of the 2062 epidemic. Its beginning is hardly noticeable, but it soon increases exponentially.

NUCLEAR MARKET
IN NEW EUROPE

Lors que soldats fureur seditieuse,
Contre leur chef feront de nuict fer luire,
Ennemy d'Albe soit par main furieuse,
Lors vexer Rome, et principaux seduire.

When soldiers mutter mutinously

Unsheathing steel at night against their chief

Albion's enemy will struggle furiously

To upset Rome, and seduce it from its principles.

Four years after England's exit from the EU [*see* 8/64 – 2064], Albion's old enemy, France, seeks to foment further discord by undermining certain aspects of the two Treaties of Rome, which, in 1957, laid the basis for what was to become the European Community. One part of the treaty was called EURATOM (European Atomic Energy Community), and dealt with the peaceful uses of atomic energy, creating a single European market for nuclear materials. The key to the quatrain, and to its nuclear element, comes in line 2, *de nuict fer luire*, which, as well as meaning to 'unsheathe one's sword at night', also means, when translated literally, both 'iron that shines at night', and 'the capacity to read at night', with the inevitable implication of energy creation. One can assume from the quatrain that 'England's enemy' is seeking to force Britain out of Europe's nuclear market once and for all.

SUMMARY

Problems flare up between England and France over nuclear matters. The root cause remains England's secession from the European Union.

WARNINGS OF GLOBAL WAR

Le fait luisant de neuf vieux eslué

Seront si grand par midi aquilon,

De sa seur propre grande alles levé.

Guyant meurdri au buisson d'ambellon.

The shining deed of the newly elected elder

Will be blown south by the great northern wind

Great halls are raised by his own sweat

Fleeing, he is killed at the bushes of Ambellon.

A precursor to the global war scenario laid out in 5/70, 9/70, 2/70, 8/70 and 3/71? The index date is right, and other clues lead us towards such a supposition, most notably the symbol of the northern wind blowing south. Most commentators have always taken *seur* in line 3 to mean *soeur*, or 'sister', but it is much more likely, if taken as an ideogram, to mean *sueur*, 'sweat'.

Guyant is most probably a misprint of the word *fuyant*, 'fleeing', but 'the bushes of Ambellon' remains a mystery. There is a clue, however. Bellona, wife of Mars, was the Roman goddess of war, and temples ('great halls') were traditionally built to her when war was in the offing. In classical literature, too, Bellona soon began to be linked to the moon-goddess of Asia, some time following the Mithridatic wars. The beaten Mithridates, of course, not wishing to fall into the hands of his enemies, found that he had so fortified himself with antidotes against poisoning by others, that he was unable to poison himself, and was finally forced to get a slave to stab him.

SUMMARY

There are rumblings of war, despite the placatory efforts of a newly elected leader.

AN ASTEROID STRIKES
THE EARTH

2069

1 / 6 9

La grand montaigne ronde de sept estades,

Apres paix, guerre, faim, innondation,

Roulera loin abysmant grands contrades,

Mesmes antiques, & grand fondation.

♉

The great mountain, seven stades around

After peace, war, hunger, flood

Will roll far, destroying great swathes of country

Even antiquities, and mighty foundations.

A *stade* was a unit of measurement equivalent to about 180 metres, so a 'mountain seven *stades* around' would measure 1,260 metres in circumference, or 1,380 yards. One presumes that Nostradamus is talking about an asteroid strike here, for we know that an asteroid of more than a kilometre in circumference, travelling at circa 30 kilometres per second, would have a humungous impact on all terrestrial life, equivalent to maybe 5,000 times the most powerful atomic warhead we possess. Tsunamis would be triggered, rising to between 300 and 800 metres above sea level. Firestorms and dust storms would circumnavigate the globe, blotting out the sun for one to two years, and disrupting food chains and breeding cycles. We can expect one such asteroid strike roughly once every 100,000 years, and Nostradamus would seem to be indicating the year 2069 as a possible strike date.

SUMMARY

Nostradamus predicts an asteroid strike in 2069, and describes the likely consequences.

GLOBAL WAR I

Des region subjectes à la Balance
Feront troubler les monts par grand guerre
Captifz tout sexe deu et tout Bisance
Qu'on criera à l'aube terre à terre.

ʊ

From the regions governed by Libra

A great war will come, enough to disturb the mountains

Both sexes will be captured, and all Byzantium

So that cries will be heard at dawn, from country
to country.

If the two countries in the Libran balance of power are the US and China, as we established in two previous quatrains, 1/54 – 2054 [US/Chinese Standoff], and 1/56 – 2056 [Islam Disturbs the Balance of World Power], then Byzantium, by which Nostradamus would appear to mean those Islamic countries once comprised within the old Ottoman Empire, will be the ember that lights the flame of global war. The war will be a nuclear one ('powerful enough to disturb mountains'), in which both men and women will fight in combat roles, particularly on the Islamic side. At the end of the war, either lamentations will be heard, or, quite possibly, the call of the *muezzin* (or 'announcer'), echoing from country to country of the subjected region.

SUMMARY

The war begins, triggered by the Islamic world. The United States and China finally face up to each other in a global arena.

GLOBAL WAR II

2070

9/70

Harnois trenchant dans les flambeaux cachez

Dedans Lyon le jour du Sacremont

Ceux de Vienne seront trestous hachez

Par les cantons Latins Mascon ne ment.

♈

Slicing armour is hidden in the torches

Inside Lyon, on the day of the sacred mountain

Those of Vienna will be put in the mincer

By the Latin cantons; Macon does not lie.

A continuation of the global war scenario Nostradamus begins in 5/70 – 2070, and completes in 3/71 – 2071. Macon is Muhammad, the name stemming from the poeticization of the name of Mecca, Muhammad's birthplace, in classical and medieval romance literature, which Nostradamus would certainly have been familiar with. 'Praised (quoth he) be Macon whom we serve.' (Fairfax *trans*: Tasso, xii. 10).

The 'mountain', in line 2, is Mount Safa, which did *not*, of course, come to Muhammad: 'If the mountain will not come to Muhammad, Muhammad must go to the mountain.' Goaded on by his followers to produce a similar miracle to those Moses and Jesus were said to have wrought in testimony to their divine authority, Muhammad, irritated at the lack of belief of his followers, devised a strategy to bring them to their senses. He called Mount Safa to him, and when it refused to come, he thanked Allah, 'because it would have fallen on us to our destruction.' Here, the implication seems to be that the Western powers have called to the mountain, and it has fallen on them, in the guise of nuclear weapons – 'slicing armour hidden in the torches'. If we cast our eyes back to quatrain 5/70, of course, we also see that the coming great war will be 'enough to disturb the mountains'.

The pun on *Vienna*, and *de Vienne*, in line 3 is also a neat one. The Congress of Vienna (1814–15), carved up Europe between the great powers, following the downfall of Napoleon, and the liaison of *de* and *vienne* gives us the French for 'become' – there will be changes to the established order, therefore, as a direct result of this conflict. It is, perhaps, useful to remember that the four great powers involved in the Congress of Vienna were Austria (the Hapsburg Empire), Britain, Prussia (the German Confederation) and Russia.

SUMMARY

Thermonuclear weapons are used on the battlefield. Whole mountains are destroyed. Efforts are made at peacemaking, but they are futile.

GLOBAL WAR III

Le dard du ciel fera son estendre,

Mors en parlant: grande execution

La pierre en l'arbre la fiere gent rendue,

Bruit humain monstre purge expiation.

༽

The spear from the skies will complete its
extinguishing

It will speak of death: a terrible execution

The proud nation will be returned to the stone
in the tree

Rumours of a human monster bring first
catharsis, then sacrifice.

This really is an extraordinary series of quatrains [10/69, 5/70, 9/70, 8/70 and 3/71], all conterminous by index date, and all with implications of nation states brought low by global thermonuclear warfare. Why have they never been linked before? The index dates are categorical, and the symbols used are unequivocal. 'The spear (or dart) from the skies will complete the extinguishing' – a wonderful description of an intercontinental missile, for *estendre* in Old French means to 'stretch', or 'spread', and *esteindre* to 'extinguish' (the 's' was later replaced by an acute accent). The concept of the 'stone in the tree' means, quite literally, to be returned to the Stone Age, in which axes were made from split branches, with sharpened celts looped in for heft. The 'human monster' takes us back once again to 3/35 – 2035 and the birth of the third Antichrist (the first two being Napoleon/Stalin and Hitler). The 'seductive' leader would, by 2070, be thirty-five years old, and in the full flow of his maturity.

SUMMARY

The war is nearly over. Unparalleled destruction has been rained upon the world. Entire countries are no more. The third Antichrist makes his move.

GLOBAL WAR IV

2070

8 / 70

Il entrera vilain, mechant, infame

Tyrannisant la Mesopotamie,

Tous amis fait d'adulterine d'ame,

Terre horrible, noir de phisonomie.

ʊ

He will enter, ugly, bad, and infamous

He will tyrannize Mesopotamia

Friends will pretend that the adulterous one has a soul

The land is horrible, and black of aspect.

Is this the 'human monster' mentioned in 2/70 – 2070 [Global War III], who will bring 'first catharsis, then sacrifice'? A better description of sycophantic expediency has never been penned than in line 3's 'friends will pretend that the adulterous one has a soul'. Mesopotamia, of course, is modern-day Iraq, with a little bit of Turkey and Syria thrown in for good measure. Not much seems to be left of this former cradle of human civilization, however, and far from living up to the meaning of its name in Greek as being the land situated 'between two rivers', it now seems more a case of its being the land situated 'between a rock and hard place'.

SUMMARY

The third Antichrist attempts to benefit from the fallout of the global war. People want to believe him. He makes his power base in what remains of the Middle East.

GLOBAL WAR V

2071

3 / 71

Ceux dans les isles de longtemps assiegez,

Prendront vigeur force contre ennemis

Ceux par dehors mors de faim profligez,

En plus grand faim que jamais seront mis.

ॐ

The islanders will face a long siege

They will defend themselves vigorously

Those outside will be assailed by hunger

It will be a far worse famine than those which
preceded it.

A direct follow-on from 5/70, 9/70, 2/70 and 8/70 – 2070 [Global War], in which the US and China go head to head in a thermonuclear contest. Nostradamus often referred to the British as 'the islanders', and given the contents of 8/64 – 2064 [Consequences of England's Secession from EU], and the implications of a British famine that is only halted by a mass return to the countryside, one could extrapolate from this that the United Kingdom remains apart from the global conflict, reverting to the Fortress Britain role that it played during World War Two. While war rages on the continent, therefore, Britain becomes self-fuelling, and self-feeding – trusting to the 'spade' [*see* my note in 8/64]. Those outside its borders face a terrible famine, but the United Kingdom, in a bid to save itself and its people, does not let them in.

SUMMARY

Britain has, for once, held itself aloof from the conflict. It now reaps the benefit. While a significant part of the rest of the world goes hungry, Britain has become self-sufficient, and manages to feed its own people.

GLOBAL WAR AFTERMATH/END OF PHOENIX PERIOD

DATE
2075

QUATRAIN
2/75

La voix ouie de l'insolite oiseau,

Sur le canon du respiral estage

Si hault viendra du froment le boisseau,

Que l'homme de l'homme fera Antropophage.

The cry of an extraordinary bird will be heard

Canoning through the air shafts

The cost of a bushel of wheat corn will soar so high

That man will make of man a cannibal.

Following on from the catastrophic global war of 2070 [5/70, 9/70, 2/70, 8/70 and 3/71], a terrible famine will devastate the earth, triggering the Change of World Order depicted in 3/79 – 2079. Birds such as crows, owls, storks, ravens and swallows were considered harbingers of either good or evil (depending on breed, colour and connotation) by the augurs of ancient Greece, but Nostradamus's use of the phrase *insolite oiseau* would seem to point us towards a rarer bird – the phoenix, for instance. For Paracelsus, the phoenix symbolized alchemy, on account of the animal's ability to change its essential form through the use of fire, and for centuries the sign of the phoenix was to be found above pharmacies and chemists' shops for that reason.

Phoenix Periods (the rare occurrences when the phoenix is actually visible to human beings) range in time from 250 years, according to Tacitus, to a maximum of 1,500 years between sightings, according to the German Egygist Lepsius. Such sightings were deemed to herald the beginnings and ends of great human eras. If we take the length of a Phoenix Period to be around 300 years, we are taken back to 1775, and the beginnings of the American War of Independence, an event that heralded both the beginnings of world revolution and the foundation of modernity. This period, Nostradamus tells us, is now at an end. Instead, we are entering an age of uncertainty and global change.

SUMMARY

The war has signalled the end of a great human era. We are entering a period of barbarism and immorality.

THIRD ANTICHRIST I

Tant attendu ne reviendra jamais

Dedans l'Europe, en Asie apparoistra

Un de la ligue issu du grand Hermes

Et sur tous rois des orientz croistra.

ॐ

The eagerly awaited one will never return

To Europe, but will reappear in Asia

One of the confederacy descended from great Hermes

He will grow above all other kings of the Orient.

One immediately thinks back to the series of quatrains dealing with the period 2032–36 [Birth of the Third Antichrist] when one reads this prophecy. The individual concerned, whose birth is described so effectively in 3/35 – 2035, would be forty years old at the time of this quatrain, and in the prime of life. It seems that he has survived the global war of 2070, and is intent on validating Nostradamus's prediction in 3/35, that 'the noise of his reputation will grow in the Eastern Kingdom' – this suggestion is further echoed in line 4 of the present quatrain, in 'he will rise above all other kings of the East'.

As if that weren't enough, we are reminded of his European origins [*see* 2/32 – 2032], and are now told that he repudiates them totally, and turns his face permanently towards the East. The 'confederacy descended from great Hermes' is of particular interest here, as it could imply a Hermetic link with Thoth (the Egyptian Hermes Trismegistus, scribe of the gods, and chief counsellor to Osiris). Either that, or a reference back to alchemy, for Hermes was the Greek Mercury, and Milton, in *Paradise Lost*, iii, 603, calls quicksilver 'volatile Hermes'. In purely classical terms, Hermes was the god of thieves, as well as being a messenger and a herald to the Olympians, and he was also the conductor of souls to Hades [*see* 6/27 – 2027: Six Lucky Gamblers]. On the whole, though, it seems most likely that Nostradamus was taking the Neo-Platonist route, as the name Trismegistus means 'thrice great', and we are dealing here with the man who may well be the third Antichrist.

SUMMARY

This is the time the third Antichrist has been waiting for. From the Middle East, he moves towards Asia, widening his power base. Nature abhors a vacuum, and the Antichrist intends to be the one to fill it.

THIRD ANTICHRIST II

L'antechrist trois bien tost anniehilez,

Vingt et sept ans sang durera sa guerre.

Les heretiques mortz, captifs, exilez.

Sang corps humain eau rougi gresler terre.

෪

The third Antichrist will soon be annihilated

His war will have lasted for twenty-seven years

The heretics are dead, captive or exiled

Human blood reddens the water that covers
the earth in hail.

Could the war Nostradamus is describing really have started in 2050, when the third Antichrist was a mere fifteen years old? [see 3/35 – 2035: Birth of the Third Antichrist]. Well, yes, it could, if the war is accepted as being one of ideological, rather than of military confrontation. There is no question here of the war having actually come to an end, but the presage in line 1 may link this quatrain to 3/79 – 2079 [Change of World Order], in which the example of the men of Phocis is summoned up to show that all is not yet lost. The final line is one of the greatest, and yet most difficult to translate, in all of Nostradamus's writings, and conjures up, in its few, almost shunted-together words, a human and nature-driven hell the like of which we haven't experienced since the last great Quaternary Ice Age of 1.6 million years ago. The original source of the image of 'blood-reddened' hail comes in Revelations 8, vii, and describes the first of the Seven Angels of God: 'The first angel sounded, and there followed hail and fire mingled with blood...'

SUMMARY

There are still some people willing to fight back against tyranny. Nostradamus describes the battle and suggests that, in the end, the third Antichrist will be beaten.

FORTRESS BRITAIN FOLLOWING GLOBAL WAR

QUATRAIN
2/77

Par arcs feux poix et par feux repoussés,
Cris hurlements sur la minuit ouis
Dedans sont mis par les remparts cassez
Par cunicules les traditeurs fuis.

༻

By arcs of fire, pitch and flame are they repulsed

Screams, cries and shouts at midnight

They are launched from inside the smashed defences

The traitors escape through their secret passages.

PREDICTION

One is tempted to see this as a continuation of the prediction from 3/71 – 2071 [Global War V], in which the UK becomes Fortress Britain once again. There is certainly the sense of a siege here, which would make sense if Britain had become self-sufficient in food, and others wished to benefit from its bounty. It seems that the British drive off the invaders, at a terrible cost, and fifth columnists and traitors escape by the very underground passages through which they sought to undermine their own people.

SUMMARY

Britain defends its borders, and its right to isolation, against outsiders and attack. Fifth columnists inside the island fail in their treason.

CIVIL DISOBEDIENCE BEGINS

QUATRAIN
10/78

Subite joie en subite tristesse

Sera à Romme aux graces embrassees

Deuil, cris, pleurs, larm, sang, excellent liesse

Contraires bandes surprinses et troussees.

ʊ

Sudden joy inside sudden sadness

Will occur at Rome, of the jealously guarded favours

Mourning, cries, tears, weeping, blood, excellent joy

Opposing groups surprised and locked up.

This is a quatrain of paradoxes. Sudden joy inside sudden sadness. Mourning, cries, tears, weeping, blood, and then the unexpected use of the Old French word *liesse*, which also means 'joy'. Opposing groups, which one takes to mean groups on both sides of the argument, are surprised and locked up. This is almost a judgment of Solomon, when one comes to think about it – the sort of response a State will give if it finds itself at an impasse, facing two opposing sides who will not, under any circumstances, compromise. What Nostradamus is describing, therefore, is the beginnings of tyranny under the guise of political expedience, which, in the light of 3/79 – 2079 [Change of World Order], will come as no surprise whatsoever.

SUMMARY

All over the world, parameters are changing. Former democratic states are arrogating despotic powers to themselves. There are mass insurrections, which are put down pitilessly.

CHANGE OF
WORLD ORDER

L'ordre fatal sempiternal par chaisne,

Viendra tourner par ordre consequent

Du port Phocen sera rompu la chaisne,

La cite prinse, l'ennemi quant et quant.

The locked and fated eternal order of things

Will switch direction, thanks to a new order

The old Greek order will be broken,

Its citadel taken; the enemy will not be accepted.

Given what Nostradamus predicts in the years both leading up to and following this quatrain, its meaning becomes all the more pivotal. It is rare for Nostradamus to generalize to such an extent, and it can only mean that he is uncertain as to the true outcome of events. Given all that, he appears to foresee what amounts to a fundamental change in the perception of democracy ('the old Greek order'). Could its 'citadel' be Athens? Or is that too literal a reading?

The 'new order' (tyranny?) does not, at the very least, find easy acceptance. Phocensian Despair, of course, means desperation which terminates in victory, and stems from the days of Philip, King of Macedon, when the men of Phocis stood alone against the united might of all their enemies. In desperation, they built an enormous pyre, meaning to immolate themselves, and their women and children, upon it. Having nothing left to lose, they then threw themselves in one final, despairing act, upon the foe, and, extraordinarily, beat them off.

SUMMARY

The old world order has changed, apparently for good. Democracy is a thing of the past. There are many who regret its passing. Having nothing left to lose, they ready themselves for a last-ditch attempt at a restoration of universal suffrage.

CLIMATE CHANGE
DUE TO GLOBAL WAR

DATE
2080

QUATRAIN
8/80

Des innocens le sang de vessue et vierge.

Tant de maulx faitz par moyen se grand Roge

Saintz simulacres tremper en ardent cierge

De frayeur crainte ne verra nul ne boge.

ʊ

The blood of innocents, of widows and virgins

The great Red One commits many evils

Holy images are infused with the light of votive candles

Terrified and fearful, people will no longer
dare to move.

Following on from the global war of 2070 [*see* 5/70, 9/70, 2/70 & 8/70 – 2070], great climatic change will come upon the world. The French, at the time Nostradamus writes, held the belief that a 'red man' commanded the elements, wrecking those he condemned to death somewhere in the seas off the coast of Brittany. Legend also has it that this same 'red man' once appeared to Napoleon in a dream, foretelling his downfall. The 'Red One', therefore, is Nostradamus's euphemism for the elements, which run amok in the aftermath of a thermonuclear war, making any form of travel impossible, and provoking, as so often happens in times of turmoil, a return to organized religion. The restoration of a communal faith was a continual preoccupation of Nostradamus's, and he returned to the subject time and time again in his writings.

SUMMARY

Fundamental climate change, triggered by the thermonuclear war of ten years back, begins to tell. People turn back to God in their uncertainty. After the horrors of an entirely man-made war, nature is now poised to take its revenge.

SUBJECT
TSUNAMI II

DATE
2080

QUATRAIN
4/80

Pres du grand fleuve, grand fosse, terre egeste,
En quinze pars sera l'eau divisee
La cité prinse, feu, sang, cris conflict mettre
Et la plus part concerne au collisee.

꒰꒱

Near the great river a ditch will form; the land
will be eaten

The water will split into fifteen channels

The city falls; fire, blood and cries conflict

Much of it caused by the collision.

When taken with 8/80 – 2080 [Climate Change Due to Global War], and 1/82 – 2082 [European Earthquakes], the 2080s do not seem like a good period to be living in southern Europe. The implication of *collisee* in the last line gives us both a 'collision', and the geographical location of the Coliseum, in Rome. A 'great river', the Tiber, runs through Rome, and Rome is situated just seventeen miles from the Tyrrhenian Sea. The Tyrrhenian Sea contains Europe's largest underwater volcano, Mount Marsili, which rears up 9,800 feet from the ocean floor. Mount Marsili was, until recently, considered dormant, but it has now been firmly established (since 1999) that the volcano is active. When Mount Marsili eventually erupts, as it most certainly will, a considerable part of the southern coast of Italy will go with it. With this in mind, quatrain 4/80 takes on a new, and far more sinister, dimension.

SUMMARY

An underwater volcano erupts beneath the Tyrrhenian Sea, causing a tsunami, which devastates the Roman peninsula.

TSUNAMI III

L'oiseau royal sur la cité solaire,

Sept mois devant fera nocturne augure

Mur d'Orient cherra tonnerre esclaire,

Sept jours aux portes les ennemis à l'heure.

ꙮ

The royal bird will fly over the city of the sun

Seven months earlier there will be a nocturnal augury

The Eastern wall will fall, amidst thunder
and lightning

For seven unremitting days the enemy
will be at the gates.

This is a direct follow-on from 4/80 – 2080 [Tsunami I], and shows just how cunningly Nostradamus linked the numbers of his quatrains and their meaning, despite their nominal appearance in entirely different *Centuries* – *Centuries* being the ten separate chapters of one hundred grouped verses (apart from *Century* 7, which contained only forty-two) that comprise the main body of Nostradamus's prophecies. In this case the link is made not only through the index numbers of 80 and 81 respectively, but also in more subtle ways.

Nostradamus mentions the 'city of the sun' in line 1 of the quatrain. This was traditionally seen as Rhodes, whose great Colossos, one of the seven wonders of the ancient world, was consecrated to Apollo, god of the sun. The final line of 4/80 reads *'et la plus part concerne au collisee.'* In that quatrain, I have taken *collisee* to mean both the Roman Coliseum, and a collision. This quatrain, with its hidden echoes of 4/80, takes the environmental disasters which befall southern Europe between the years 2080 and 2082, even further south. The 'royal bird' is the ibis, sacred to Egypt, a country situated just 400 miles due south of Rhodes – to kill an ibis was a capital offence.

The implication here is that both Rhodes and Egypt are linked in an environmental catastrophe, whose origin stems from the shattering of the 'Eastern Wall'. The fallout from the catastrophe will continue for seven days, just as the augury occurred seven months earlier, and just as there were seven wonders of the ancient world, which included the Colossus, and seven wonders of the middle ages, which included the Coliseum. Seven, of course, is a holy number, and Levitical purifications, of which this tsunami may be seen as one, traditionally lasted for seven days.

SUMMARY

Another tsunami devastates the Aegean area around the island of Rhodes, causing havoc on the Turkish mainland.

NEW LEADER APPEARS

Le grand crier sans honte audacieux,

Sera esleu gouverneur de l'armee

La hardiesse de son contentieux,

Le pont rompu cité de peur pasmee.

ʊ

The great scolder, bold and shameless

Will be elected head of the army

The boldness of his contentions

Will cause the bridge to break and the city to
faint with fear.

This quatrain comes bang in the middle of three terrible years in which the world order changes, and in which nature, twisted and suborned by man to his own ends, finally wreaks its revenge upon the world. This period throws up a special sort of leader – a man who harangues and scolds his people until they finally elect him head of the army. It is natural for people to seek strong leadership at a time of uncertainty, and this man provides that leadership. Coming so soon after 3/79 – 2079 [Change of World Order], this quatrain could almost be viewed as an optimistic one, despite the worrying implications in the last line. With what nature has in store for the world, firm leadership will become a necessity.

SUMMARY

A strong new leader, who is, nonetheless, benevolent, comes to the fore. People, searching for miracles, turn to him. He is only a man, however, and cannot turn back the clock.

EUROPEAN EARTHQUAKE

QUATRAIN
1/82

Quand les colomnes de bois grande tremblée,
D'auster conduicte couverte de rubriche,
Tant vuidera dehors une grande assemblée,
Trembler Vienne et le pays d'Austriche.

℧

When even the trees shake mightily

And the south wind seems covered in blood

So many will try to escape

That Vienna and all Austria will shake
with their passing.

Nostradamus's use of the word 'shake' on two separate occasions in this quatrain gives us our clue. An earthquake, of a sufficient magnitude to make even the greatest trees tremble, will strike central Europe, with its epicentre possibly near, or inside, the Czech Republic. The western part of the Bohemian Massif is well known for its earthquake swarms, with more than 8,000 separate quakes recorded in the period between 1985 and 1986, just one hundred years before Nostradamus's predicted date for the big one. The dust from the quake will filter and transform the sun's rays until they seem 'covered in blood', and there will be a mass exodus on such a scale that even Vienna, situated a scant few miles from the Czech border, will 'shake with their passing'. When, in addition, we take into account quatrain 8/80 – 2080 [Climate Change Due to Global War], with its index date of 2080, the pattern begins to fall even more firmly into place.

SUMMARY

Natural disasters, triggered by the global war, continue. An earthquake strikes the Czech Republic. Its power is so great that aftershocks are felt as far away as Austria.

LOCUST PLAGUE

Friens, Antibor, villes autour de Nice,

Seront vastees fort par mer et par terre

Les saturelles terre et mer vent propice,

Prins, morts, troussez, pillés, sans loi de guerre.

ℰℐ

Fréjus, Antibes, and the towns around Nice

Will be devastated both by land and by sea

Locusts will come on propitious winds

Kidnap, death, rape, pillage, no martial law.

More natural disasters for this apocalyptic three-year period (2080–82). If anyone ever doubted that Nostradamus's quatrains were linked across the different *Centuries* in which they appear, then the last few predictions, all relating to natural disasters, and all occurring within three years of his index dates in *Centuries* 8, 4, 5, 1 and 3, should convince them otherwise. The Mediterranean, to put it bluntly, is in for it. Tsunamis, earthquakes, climate change – all contrive to create a new environment – a new landscape, almost – in which the coastal borders of Europe are perpetually at risk. In the bare few lines of this quatrain, an entire story emerges of dreadful storms, followed by a plague of locusts, followed by a total collapse of law and order, in which people go, quite literally, mad, and only the strong, or the wicked, can survive. It comes as no surprise to find that, just three years after these events, the French state is entering a long-term period of crisis [10/85 – 2085].

SUMMARY

Climatic conditions trigger a plague of locusts, but on an unprecedented scale. The French Riviera is particularly hard hit when the locusts are borne over from North Africa on freak winds.

US EARTHQUAKE

Sol vingt de Taurus si fort terre trembler
Le grand theatre rempli ruinera
L'air ciel et terre obscurcir et troubler
Lors l'infidelle Dieu et sainctz voguera.

♈

When the sun is at twenty degrees in Taurus,
a great earthquake

Will totally destroy the packed Great Theatre

Air, sky and earth will be murky and unsettled

So that even infidels will call on God and the
saints to steer them.

The years 2080 to 2084, encapsulated in an index-conjoined series of quite remarkable quatrains, seem among the bleakest that mankind will ever have to go through. Earthquakes, tsunamis, locust plagues and radical climate change will harry the world as a result of our own actions, and there will be a mass return to organized religion [*see* also 8/80 – 2080: Climate Change Due to Global War].

The next Jupiter in Taurus square to Neptune in Leo will occur in 2083. The last occurred in June 1929, a few months before the great October Wall Street Crash, which ushered in a ten-year period of unmitigated disaster for all the Western economies, and, in particular, for the United States. Nostradamus speaks specifically here of a terrible earthquake which will destroy what he calls the 'Great Theatre'. Could the 'Great Theatre' be Wall Street?

SUMMARY

Parts of New York are destroyed by an earthquake. The fall of the great buildings creates such a dense pall of smoke, dust and debris, that for a long time the rescue and emergency services find it impossible to function.

AFTERMATH OF THE COMING OF THE THIRD ANTICHRIST

2084

5/84

Naistra du gouffre & cité immesuree,
Nay de parents obscure & ténébreux:
Qui la puissance du grand roi reveree,
Voudra destruire par Rouan & Evreux.

༽༼

He will be born of the pit and of the immeasurable city

Product of dark and infernal parents

Who wish the power of the great and revered king

To be destroyed by Rouen and Evreux.

PREDICTION

This would appear to be yet another third Antichrist quatrain, with a probable date of 2084 – the wording is so severe, and the reference to the infernal regions so specific, that it appears to be a natural follow-on to the sequence of disasters foretold in the quatrains describing the years 2080–84, and predates the French Crisis sequence that starts in 2085.

SUMMARY

Another in the infernal chain of quatrains describing the catastrophic years 2080–84.

THE FINAL POPE

Roi exposé parfaira l'hecatombe,

Apres avoir trouvé son origine,

Torrent ouvrir de marbre & plomb la tombe

D'un grand Romain d'enseigne Medusine.

ℰ

The king makes a statement completing the hecatomb

After having discovered its origin

A flood of marble and lead opens the tomb

Of a great Roman of the Medusan persuasion.

The Roman of the 'Medusan persuasion' is, obviously, mortal, as that was the only way in which Medusa differed from her other two Gorgon sisters – it is also, presumably, why he ended up in a 'hecatomb'. The puns and allusions continue with the mention of 'marble' in line 3, evoking the Medusan curse of turning things to stone. This, in turn, brings to mind the name Peter, the first pope (Matthew xvi, 18: 'I also say to you that you are Peter, and upon this rock I will build my Church'). Also in line 3, the adjunctive 'lead' suggests alchemical transmutation (i.e. one thing turning into another). No pope has ever adopted the name Peter II, yet St Malachy's *Prophecy of the Popes* (published in 1595, almost thirty years after Nostradamus's death) names a certain Peter the Roman, or *Petrus Romanus*, as the final pope. Given the diabolical events of 2080–84, the end year of this period seems a reasonable choice for the death of the last pope of the Catholic Church.

SUMMARY

Following on from the disastrous events predicted between 2080 and 2084, the death of St Malachy's *Petrus Romanus*, the last ever pope, might very well occur in this year.

FRENCH CRISIS
PRELUDE I

DATE
2085

QUATRAIN
10/85

Le vieil tribun au point de la trebemide.
Sera pressee captif ne deslivrer,
Le veuil non veuil ne mal parlant timide
Par legitime à ses amis livrer.

ೲ

The old demagogue, salt measure teetering

Will be urged never to release the captive

The old man, though not weak, does not wish
to be maligned

By legitimate means he delivers him to his friends.

Quatrain 10/98 – 2098 [French Crisis I] deals with the symbolical significance of 'salt', both as a concept of the vigour of the State, when the salt is kept neatly sealed up, and as an evil omen, when it is spilled or wasted. This quatrain predates that one by exactly thirteen years (thirteen is an unlucky number – traditionally, in the city of Paris, no house bears it; it was also the number present at the Last Supper, in which Judas upset the salt shaker), and points to what may have caused the French Crisis in the first place.

Trémie, in Old French, is a mill-hopper, or salt measure, and also carries with it the implication of shaking, which is generally seen as an adjunct to old age. *Vieil*, *veuil* and *veule* mean, respectively, 'old', 'wishes' and 'weak', all, once again, leading us towards the image of an elderly leader, without vigour, unsure of his ground, and minding overmuch what is said about him. The identity of the mysterious 'captive' is unclear, but it is perhaps apposite to point out that the third Antichrist spoken of in 3/35 – 2035 would be just fifty years old at the time of this quatrain.

SUMMARY

A crisis has been brewing in France. Now it comes to a head. The aged leader hesitates, uncertain how to respond. This is a fatal mistake.

THE FUTURE OF ISRAEL

Le vieux plain barbe soubs le statut severe,

A Lyon faict dessus l'Aigle Celtique

Le petit grand trop autre persevere,

Bruit d'arme au ciel: mer rouge Ligustique.

ᘒ

The old man conceals stern laws beneath his beard

The Lion is raised above the wedge-shaped Eagle

The great man, small in size, persists too long

There is the sound of weapons from the sky:
the Red Sea turns Ligurian.

An extraordinary quatrain, persistently mistranslated. Suffice it to say that the 'lion' is the emblem of the tribe of Judah (i.e. Israel). 'Judah is a lion's whelp: ... he couched as a lion, and as an old lion; who shall rouse him up?' (Genesis xlix, 9.). The 'eagle', on the other hand, was the ensign of the ancient kings of Babylon and Persia, of the Ptolemies and Seleucides. Another link to the world of Islam is the mention of the Red Sea, which is the geographical centre of the Islamic world, running, as it does, near to the holy centres of Medina and Mecca. This is so categorical, that it comes as some surprise to find that no commentator has yet made the connection.

Perhaps it is the mention of Liguria which has traditionally lured commentators towards Italy, and away from the Middle East? But the great E. Cobham Brewer tells us that the Ligurian arts were traditionally those of deception and trickery, and this is the meaning which Nostradamus and his contemporaries would have derived from the last line. Given all this, the quatrain now begins to make sense. A literal translation would read as follows: 'The leader of Israel is a hard taskmaster / His people have the ascendancy over the Arabs / But he does not know when to stop / The Arabs resort to trickery: a terrible war ensues.'

SUMMARY

Israel has still not resolved the Arab problem. Both sides find it impossible to forget or forgive the past. A forceful Israeli leader takes the initiative, triggering a fresh war.

CYPRUS PARTITION

En ce temps là sera frustree Cypres,

De son secours de ceux de mer Egee

Vieux trucidez, mais par mesles et lyphres

Seduict leur Roy, Royne plus outragee.

〰

At this time Cyprus will be frustrated

In its desire for aid from the Greeks

The old will be snuffed out, both by cannon and
by distress

Their king will be seduced, their queen even
more affronted.

The Turkish invasion of Cyprus in 1974 led to the occupation of over a third of Cypriot territory by the Turks, who had ruled the island in its totality from 1571 to 1878. If one also bears in mind that the Greeks, the Ptolemies, the Romans, the Byzantines, the Franks, the Arabs, the Venetians, and the British had all ruled the island at some time or other in its 4,000-year history, it seems that Cyprus has always been something of an Aegean powder keg.

It's no surprise, therefore, that trouble springs up again in the latter part of the twenty-first century. King Constantine II of Greece was deposed by a military junta in 1973, and Greek republican status was ratified by the electorate after civilian rule was restored in 1974, coinciding almost exactly with their partial loss of sovereignty over Cyprus. Greek history is full of surprises and upsets, and it would not stretch logic to foresee a return to a monarchy at some point during the twenty-first century. The former King Constantine himself has never given up his claim to the throne, and his heir, Crown Prince Paul, was born in 1967, while Paul's eldest son, Constantino, was born in 1999 – so the succession seems assured.

SUMMARY

Cyprus still occupies the minds of the Greeks and of the Turks. The Greeks, their monarchy and self-confidence restored, attempt to reverse the partition.

US & CHINA SEE
EYE TO EYE

2089

2/89

Un jour seront demis les deux grands maistres,

Leur grand pouvoir se verra augmenter

La terre neufue sera en ses hauts estres,

Au sanguinaire le nombre racompté.

One day the two great leaders will become friends

Their great power will become greater

The new world will be at its highest point

The number shall be told to the red one.

It's quite encouraging to learn that after the global war of 2070, and the environmental horrors of the 2080s, human nature, in the form of personal friendship, can still make a difference. The two great leaders, of course, will be those of China and the US, and the influence of the New World (North America) will have peaked. The Great Red One has already appeared in 8/80 – 2080 [Climate Change Due to Global War], and the telling to him of the number 'two', does not bode well. We already know about the evil implications the number two can have numerologically, from 4/59 – 2059 [Buddhism & the Protestant Church], and the linking of this number with the 'red man' who commands the elements is far from auspicious. However, it would be churlish to dilute the glory of one of Nostradamus's few partially optimistic quatrains just because of the sting in the tail of the last line.

SUMMARY

Their confidence shaken by the long-term fallout from the global war of 2070, the new leaders of the United States and China offer each other the hand of friendship. Peace reigns for a while.

HUNGARY IN CRISIS

2090

2/90

Par vie et mort changé regne d'Ongrie
La loi sera plus aspre que service
Leur grand cité d'hurlements plaincts et crie
Castor et Pollux ennemis dans la lice.

༄

Life and death change the rule of Hungary

Law becomes more asper than duty

Their great city rings with cries and laments

Castor and Pollux confront each other in the lists.

The *aspre* ('asper') was an ancient Turkish coin, equal to about the 120th part of a *piastre* ('piaster'). 'Castor and Pollux', the twin sons of Leda, and brothers to Helen and Clytemnestra, were known to sailors as comazants when they appeared, in the guise of St Elmo's Fire, at the mastheads of ships. If only one flame appeared, the Romans called it Helen, and believed that it portended that the worst of the storm was still to come, but if two flames appeared, they were Castor and Pollux, and it meant that the storm was over.

The reference to 'lists' (the barriers set up for medieval jousting tourneys) in line 4 (*lice* can also mean 'bitch' in Old French, but we can discount this) is a reference to the horses of Castor and Pollux, Cyllaros and Harpagus, which they mounted on their return from the infernal regions, and on which Nostradamus pictures them doing battle – the implication being that if only one of them survives, the worst of the crisis is yet to come, but that if both come out of the contest equally, the crisis will be over.

SUMMARY

Hungary faces a short and sharp crisis. An unlikely concatenation of disparate forces resolves it, much to everyone's surprise.

GREEK NUCLEAR ACCIDENT

DATE
2090

QUATRAIN
5/90

Dans les cyclades, en perinthe et larisse
Dedans Sparte tout le Pelloponesse
Si grand famine, peste par faux connisse
Neuf mois tiendra et tout le chevronesse.

℧

In the Cyclades, and in Perinthus and Larissa

In Sparta, and all through the Peloponnese

A terrible famine, a plague of false dust

Nine months it will last, patterning everything.

Nine is one of the great mystical numbers (along with five and three), and corresponds to the *diapason*, the *diapente* and the *diatron* of the ancient Greeks – the trinity of trinities, in other words. This stems from the concept of man as a full chord of eight notes, and the Deity, at least according to Pythagoras, taking the ninth place on the scale, i.e. perfection. This concept of nine carries through nearly all cultures, and corresponds, needless to say, with the normal length, in months, of a human pregnancy. Both the Etruscans and the Sabines had nine major gods apiece, and the medieval earth was supposed to rest at the centre of nine spheres, above which came the Primum Mobile, or Heaven of Heavens.

All this to say that Nostradamus, when he speaks of a 'plague of false dust', is most probably talking of an act of God, rather than any man-made catastrophe. A worse-than-normal Melteme wind, triggered by global warming, springs to mind. [*See* also 2/3 – 2103: Global Warming/ Mediterranean Famine].

SUMMARY

At some time during the preceding years, the Greeks have acquired a number of nuclear reactors. There is a meltdown of one reactor, causing a Chernobyl-like tragedy. The fallout from the disaster lingers for nine months, afflicting both the living and the as yet unborn.

TWENTY YEARS SINCE
END OF GLOBAL WAR

DATE
2091

QUATRAIN
1 / 91

Les dieux feront aux humains apparance,

Ce qu'ils seront auteurs de grand conflict

Avant ciel veu serein espee et lance,

Que vers main gauche sera plus grand afflit.

ʊ

It will seem to human beings that the gods

Must have been the authors of the great war

Once, long ago, the sky was clear of weapons

Whereas now, on the left hand, there is damage
still to come.

It is now twenty years since the end of the 2070–71 global war [5/70, 9/70, 2/70, 8/70 & 3/71], and the long-term fallout – emotional, ecological and thermonuclear – is still being felt. The war was so terrible that it seems to many observers as if non-human forces must have been involved in its inception. People look back nostalgically to a serene time when the skies were clear of hardware and tactical weapons, and, presumably, full of birds.

Nostradamus would have had no concept of the existence of either a left or a right wing in terms of politics, but he would have known, from his reading of Plato, Plutarch and Aristotle, that the left was the side of evil omens and of sinister actions, and that any signs seen over the left shoulder were considered particularly bad auspices by the Greek and Roman augurs, who reputedly studied the flight of birds for signs of future trends.

SUMMARY

Twenty years after the end of the global war, the great powers come together at a conference to consider its implications for the future of the planet. People regret the passing of the old days, and fear that further conflict is imminent.

FRENCH CRISIS PRELUDE II

La regne à deux laissé bien peu tiendront

Trois ans sept mois passés feront la guerre

Les deux vestales contre eux rebelleront

Victor puis nay en Armorique terre.

༽༼

Their joint rule won't last long

In three years and seven months time they
will go to war

The two virgins will rebel against them

The victor is later born on American soil.

This is a categorical precursor to the French Crisis that occurs in 2098, even down to the very precise date of 'three years and seven months' ahead. The two virgins in line 3 are Joan of Arc, the spirit of French national pride [*see* 10/98 – 2098: French Crisis I], and Marianne, the girl with the Phrygian cap seen on French monuments, stamps and coins, and the symbol of both Republican France and freedom from oppression (the Phrygian cap was worn by freed slaves in Roman times).

The last line is a baffler, though. Why should the victor be born only later, on American soil? *Armorique* can also mean Brittany, but that doesn't get us much further. Unless we take America to mean 'the land of the free', and take the 'victor' to be symbolically born of one, or both, of the virgins? That would mean that the true spirit of France will be recreated in the Americas, and one is then thrown back onto French separatist Canada, and the possibilities of an independent Francophile state surrounding Quebec.

SUMMARY

Trouble is still brewing in France, despite the election of a coalition government. There are fears for the future of French culture, although the Francophone outpost in Canada affords some hope.

ECOLOGICAL BURN-OUT

Les lieux peuplez seront inhabitables
Pour champs avoir grand division
Regnes livrez à prudents incapables
Lors les grands freres mort et dissention.

ʊ

Formerly inhabited lands will become unfit
for human life

Cultivable fields will be divided up

Power will be given to overcautious fools

From that moment on, death and discord for
the great brothers.

The great brothers are *Liberté, Égalité* and *Fraternité* (Freedom, Equality and Brotherhood), symbols of the revolutionary French Republic, and known historically as the Declaration of the Rights of Man and of the Citizen. This would tend to link the quatrain to the French Crisis of 2098–2101, except that the verse would seem to point towards an ecological, rather than an overtly political, crisis. It's possible, of course, that the land reform mentioned in line 2 forms part of the fuse that eventually triggers the constitutional upheaval, but the global nature of line 1 might incline us to veer away from a purely parochial reading. Line 3 is a stunner, and could be applied to almost all governments and their incumbents, and is surely worthy of use as a one-off epigraph in its own right.

SUMMARY
The ecological fallout from the global war of 2070 continues, with swathes of the world left virtually uninhabitable. The quality of leadership, though, in the aftermath of the crisis, leaves something to be desired.

SECULARIZATION
OF A SUPERSTATE

Celui qu'aura la charge de destruire
Templus et sectes, changez par fantaisie
Plus aux rochiers qu'aux vivans viendra nuire,
Par langue ornee d'oreilles resasie.

ↄ

The man whose duty it is to destroy

Fantasy-driven temples and sects

Will confine himself to the inanimate

And to those whose ears are filled with vainglory.

PREDICTION

Who could this be? The pope? Or someone whom a nominally secular superstate commissions to eradicate dissent? Either way, it seems we are dealing with a fundamentally decent person who destroys stones rather than human beings. It's a worrying quatrain, though, and one cannot help wondering whether, rather as in Russia under Stalin, the state in question is not trying to eradicate religion in its entirety.

SUMMARY

An effort is made to eradicate religion by one of the great world powers. The scale is similar to Stalin's secularization of Russia during the 1930s and 1940s, although this tyrant seems content to destroy buildings rather than people.

THE EMERGENCE OF A NEW RELIGIOUS SECT

2096

10/96

Religion du nom des mers vaincra,

Contre le secte fils Adaluncatif,

Secte obstinee deploree craindra,

Des deux blessez par Aleph & Aleph.

ↄ

A religion with the name of the sea will win

Against the sect of the bound and captive son

This obstinate and much deplored sect will live in fear

Of the two injured by Aleph & Aleph.

The word *caitif* is Old French for a captive or wretched person, and *adalligo* is the Latin for to bind or fasten to – put both words together, and you have a fair definition for a word (*Adaluncatif*) that has baffled Nostradamian commentators for centuries. *Aleph* is the first letter of the Hebrew alphabet, just as *Alif* is that of the Arabic – could the sect mentioned be in opposition to both? The 'bound and captive son' is, of course, Jesus Christ, and so what Nostradamus appears to be suggesting is that a new sect comes to the fore, sidelining Christianity, but still fearing it. The clue and the dating for this quatrain may lie in its analogous counterpart, 1/96 – 2096: Secularization of a Superstate.

SUMMARY

The year is 2096. Sects and cults are pretty much universal. Nostradamus foresees a clash between the established religions of Islam and Judaism, and a new sect, named after the sea (the Atlanteans?).

THE MIDDLE EAST

Nouvelle loi terre neufve occuper,

Vers la Syrie, Judee et Palestine

Le grand empire barbare corruer,

Avant que Phoebus son siecle determine.

ꙮ

New laws will rule new lands

Towards Syria, Judea and Palestine

The great barbarian empire will decay

Before Phoebus concludes his dominance
of the century.

Phoebus is the sun. In Greek mythology Apollo was called Phoebos, the sun god, after the act of 'shining'. He was regarded as the font of moral excellence, and his influence was a benevolent one. The implication here is that moral and ethical laws are overturned in the Middle East, and one is forced to refer back to 2/85 – 2085 [The Future of Israel] for an explanation. The 'great barbarian empire' is possibly that of Israel, therefore, when one takes into account the meaning of the word 'barbarian' in its biblical sense (and we are talking of the Bible lands here). 'Therefore if I know not the meaning of the voice, I shall be unto him that speaketh a barbarian, and he that speaketh shall be a barbarian unto me.' [I Corinthians xiv, 11].

Yet another reading could have the Arab world as the barbarian empire, with each side refusing to hear the other's voice. A third reading gives us the word barbarian in its literal, and Latinate sense, as the 'bearded one'. German legend has it that Charles V, with his crown and sceptre, and with all his knights and vassals surrounding him, still lives inside the Wunderberg, on the great moor near Salzburg, haunt of the Wild-women. His grey beard has twice encircled the royal table, and when it grows long enough to encircle it three times, the Antichrist will appear.

SUMMARY

The Middle East remains tinder dry, and cracks are appearing in the entrenched positions of both parties.

FRENCH CRISIS I

2098

10/98

La splendeur claire à pucelle joyeuse
Ne luyra plus, long temps sera sans sel,
Avec marchans, ruffiens, loups oudieuse,
Tous pesle mesle montre universel.

ৎৢ

The redolent ashes of the joyful virgin

Will darken; for a long time there will be no salt

Black marketeers, ruffians, and odious wolves

Pell-mell everywhere.

Jeanne la Pucelle (Joan of Arc) was, at least according to French legend, burnt by the English, at Rouen, for sorcery, in 1431. Nostradamus's use of the Old French word *claire*, meaning ashes or bones traditionally used in refining, pinpoints the exact identity of the virgin he is alluding to, and, in addition, allows for an amusing pun on her importance as an icon of the French State – from clarity to darkness, in other words.

The entire quatrain is filled with such paradoxes, as we also have the use of the word 'salt' in line 2, which can mean either food, or, more likely in this context, 'vigour', as in Shakespeare's *Othello*, iii, 3, when Iago refers to it as '...hot as monkeys, salt as wolves in pride.' In Leonardo da Vinci's great portrait *The Last Supper*, Judas Iscariot is known by the salt cellar knocked over by his arm, an occurrence that is almost universally acknowledged as a bad omen. Thus, when the salt of a country (France) is spilled, and its spirit (Joan of Arc) is lost, free rein is offered to every form of charlatan and trickster to use the place as his playground. In this context the word 'playground' is used advisedly, since pell-mell is an ancient Italian game, stemming from *palla*/ball and *maglia*/bat, as well as its later, more common meaning, of to sink into reckless confusion.

SUMMARY

The French State, fragile for some time now, erupts into major crisis. Chaos ensues, and France loses itself in anarchy.

FRENCH CRISIS II

2099

6/99

L'ennemi docte se tournera confus,
Grand camp malade, et de faict par embusches,
Monts Pyrenees et Poenus lui seront faicts refus
Proche du fleuve decouvrant antiques cruches.

ℰ

The learned enemy will turn about in confusion

The mighty army sickens, brought low by ambush

Both the hills of the Pyrenees and of the Apennines
will be closed to him

Old containers will be discovered near the river.

A follow on, perhaps, to 10/98 – 2098 [French Crisis I]? There is an echo of biological warfare here, as the 'mighty army sickens', and sinister-sounding 'old containers' are found near a river – however this may just as well be meant metaphorically, the 'mighty army' implying past glories, and the 'sickening' being one of the soul. It is also possible that the 'learned enemy' in line 1 is linked to the 'enemy' in 10/1 – 2101 [French Crisis IV], who doesn't keep his part of the treaty. In this case, all four quatrains must be taken together to form a worrying whole for the French State.

SUMMARY

The French crisis intensifies, and the army is called in. The intervention is ineffective, and the crisis worsens.

FRENCH CRISIS III

Longtemps au ciel sera veu gris oiseau,

Aupres de Dole et de Touscane terre

Tenant au bec un verdoyant rameau,

Mourra tost grand et finera la guerre.

༄

For a long time a grey bird will be seen

High above Dôle and Tuscany

Holding in its beak a flowering branch

The great one will soon die, and the war shall end.

PREDICTION

The grey bird is an arrow, winged with grey goose feathers: 'The grey goose wing was the death of him,' goes the ancient proverb. A dove, representing the human soul, traditionally flew from the mouths of saints at their death. The death foretold is probably that which occurs in 10/1 – 2101 [French Crisis IV]. An alternative reading would have the grey bird as the dove of peace, holding an olive branch in its mouth – the dove, in conventional Christian iconography, signifies the Holy Ghost.

SUMMARY

One of the leaders who triggered the French crisis is about to die. His death will bring peace.

FRANCO-BRITISH CRISIS

Dedans les isles si horrible tumulte

Bien on n'orra qu'une bellique brigue

Tant grand sera des predateurs l'insulte

Qu'on se viendra ranger à la grand ligne.

ℒ

A horrible tumult in the islands

Soon only the warlike cabal will be heard

So great will be the predators' insults

That a great league will form against them.

Given the French Crisis described in 10/98, 6/99, 1/100 & 10/1 – 2098–2101, and given France's proximity to the United Kingdom, and given the fact that Nostradamus habitually referred to the British Isles as 'the islands', it doesn't exactly beggar the imagination to suppose that the 'predator', in this case, might be France. If, in addition, we take into account the very specific mention of Joan of Arc, in 10/98, and the long-term grudge held by the French against the English for her alleged burning at Rouen (other French sources have her marrying the Sieur des Armoise, at Metz, with whom she went on to have a family), then the likelihood becomes even greater. Nostradamus is not, of course, implying that France is going to invade Britain, or any such nonsense, but merely that there will be a severe falling out between the two ancient rivals. When one remembers that England acrimoniously seceded from the European Union in 2060 [see 8/60], then this quatrain makes all the more sense.

SUMMARY

France, irritated by its own problems, turns its attentions to external matters, in an effort to placate its people. A rift is contrived between France and the United Kingdom.

FRENCH CRISIS IV

2101

10 / 1

A l'ennemy l'ennemy foi promise
Ne se tiendre les captifs retenus
Prins preme mort et le rest en chemise,
Damné le reste pour estre soustenus.

ʊ

A treaty between enemies

Is not kept: the captives are not released

The leader is captured and killed, his remains
are stripped

The rest are damned for sustaining him.

PREDICTION

We're a very long way from home here, and apart from translating the quatrain as accurately as possible, it is very difficult to tease out a precise prediction. The quatrain is so close in time to the last three, that they are almost certainly connected.

SUMMARY

Despite its efforts at diluting its domestic problems by means of a contrived spat with the United Kingdom, France is finally forced to face up to the root cause of the recent crisis. One of the main protagonists is dead – the other is brought down too, despite his last-ditch attempts at trickery.

GLOBAL WARMING IV/ MEDITERRANEAN FAMINE

Pour la chaleur solaire sus la mer

De Negrepont les poissons demi cuits

Les habitans les viendront entamer

Quand Rhod, et Gennes leur faudra le biscuit.

ᘒ

Due to the sun overheating the sea

The fish from Negroponte will be parboiled

The local inhabitants will claim them

While people in Rhodes and Genoa are starving.

Negroponte was the Venetian name for Evvoia (Euboea), a Greek island in the Aegean Sea famed for its sulphur springs. Like Rhodes and Genoa, it changed hands numerous times during the course of history, and it is perhaps this which provides the connection Nostradamus is seeking – mention, however, must also be made of the village of 'Gennes' in France, on the Loire river, a few miles to the north of Saumur, but it would probably be tendentious in the extreme to try to engineer some extreme connection between there, the Ligurian Sea, and the Aegean.

If we accept the first reading of Genoa, then, it seems that Nostradamus is describing a catastrophical increase in global warming, to the extent that a relatively shallow sea like the Aegean (at least where it shelves towards the land), actually begins to boil its own fish. The word *entamer*, too, is an interesting one, because, as well as to encroach on a person's rights, it can also mean to make a cut or a graze in the flesh, both symbolically and in real life. Putting all these disparate elements together, *à la* Sherlock Holmes, we are left with a dreadful scene of starvation and privation, which the islanders of Evvoia refuse to alleviate.

SUMMARY

After a disastrously hot summer in the Aegean area, crops are spoiled, and there is widespread famine. The shallower parts of the Mediterranean become like pea soup, and fish, with nowhere to escape to, are parboiled in the heat.

SUBMARINE WARFARE

Quand dans poisson fer et lettre enfermée

Hors sortira qui pis fera la guerre

Aura par mer sa classe bien ramée,

Apparoissant près de Latin terre.

℧

When a letter is enclosed inside an iron fish

The man who emerges is entitled to make war

His fleet will travel beneath the boughs of the sea

Reappearing near a Latin land.

The key word in this quatrain is *ramée*, which, in Old French, means 'beneath the boughs' or 'under the trees', with the emphasis being on something which 'shelters'. When this is conjoined with 'the sea', and an 'iron fish', what Nostradamus is talking about becomes pretty obvious – a fleet of submarines. The Latin land is probably Latin America, although it could equally well apply to Spain or Italy.

SUMMARY

A diplomatic crisis is triggered at the United Nations. A fleet of submarines is sent to quell the disturbance, with permission to make war if the situation warrants it.

NOSTRADAMUS TAKES HIS LEAVE

Vingt ans du regne de la lune passez,
Sept mil ans autre tiendra sa monarchie,
Quand le soleil prendra ses jours laissez,
Lors accomplit a fine ma Prophecie.

ꙮ

Twenty years after the moon's reign is over

Another monarch will take over for seven
thousand years

When the sun finally takes its leave

My prophesying will be accomplished.

The moon (*mòna*) in Anglo-Saxon means a 'measurer' of time. In Sanskrit, Gothic, Old French and Greek, the moon was viewed in a similar way, and in the true tradition of the functionality of right-brain (insight, imagination, musicality, art awareness, 3-D forms, left-hand control) and left-brain (reasoning, science, language, number skills, right-hand control), it was considered a masculine and left-brained, rather than a feminine and right-brained, force by, amongst others, the Arabians, the Slavs, the Hindus, the Mexicans and the Lithuanians.

The sun, on the other hand, and particularly in Celtic and low-Breton mythology, took on a feminine aspect, and lived in perpetual fear of being eaten by the wolf Fenris (hence eclipses). The Celts believed that the sun would one day have a daughter, who would reign in her stead, rekindling the life force of a weary world. John Donne has this to say about the duality of the sun and moon:

> *Here lyes a shee Sunne, and a hee Moone here,*
> *She gives the best light to his Spheare,*
> *Or each is both, and all, and so*
> *They unto one another nothing owe...'*
>
> **[An Epithalamion on the Lady Elizabeth and**
> **Count Palatine, vii, 1–4].**

Nostradamus is now telling us that we have come to the end of that particular era of Manichean dualism, and that we must prepare ourselves for Armageddon, and a subsumation into Haeckelean Monism, or the Universal All. The End, in other words.

SUMMARY

The human period in world affairs is coming to an end. It has lasted for a very short time, and will leave no imprint whatsoever upon its passing. Nature will fill the vacuum left by humanity.

THE GREAT COMEDIAN

Le temps present avecques le passé

Sera iugé par grand Iovialiste,

Le monde tard lui sera lasse,

Et desloial par le clergé iuriste.

༒

Time present and time past

Will be judged by the great comedian

The world will tire of him when it is too late

Having forsaken its conventional clergy.

With its index date of 73, and its apocalyptic content, this is clearly a run-up to Nostradamus's End of Days quatrain, number 10/74 – 1774: Armageddon/The Final Prophecy. The poet T. S. Eliot obviously had the present quatrain in mind when he wrote as the opening lines to 'Burnt Norton' (the first of the *Four Quartets*):

> *Time present and time past*
> *Are both perhaps present in time future,*
> *And time future contained in time past.*
> *If all time is eternally present,*
> *All time is unredeemable.*

Nostradamus's sensational image of the 'great comedian' also tallies with his End of Days quatrain, for lines 1 and 2 of 10/74 read: 'When the great number seven completes itself/ Games will begin at the Tomb side.'

Here he foresees the run-up to Armageddon as reflected in the loss of mankind's interest in 'conventional' religion. Enlightenment, as always, comes too late, and the 'great comedian' (whom we may reasonably assume to be Satan) snatches the pot.

SUMMARY

Human beings have forsaken religion in favour of pleasure and instant gratification. The devil has won. In the next quatrain Nostradamus imagines Satan cutting a caper at the side of mankind's universal tomb.

ARMAGEDDON/
THE FINAL PROPHECY

DATE
7074

QUATRAIN
10/74

Au revolu du grand nombre septiesme,

Apparoistra au temps jeux d'Hecatombe,

Non esloigné de grand d'age milliesme,

Que les entrez sortiront de leur tombe.

ᘔ

When the great number seven completes itself

Games will begin at the Tomb side

Not far from the turn of the Millennium

The dead will rise out of their graves.

Seven is the holy number, and equates, symbolically, with a span of length – the beginning and the end of things. Just as there are seven ages in the life of man, and seven bodies in alchemy, and seven spirits of God, so there have been seven great eras in the life of the earth. These are now over.

Nostradamus's use of the word *jeux* (games) in line 2 is an odd one, but then we remember the Greek concept of the playfulness of the gods [*see* 8/16 – 2016: Ecological Disasters II], and the image is no longer so surprising. The final dating of Armageddon presents some difficulties, as we do not know if Nostradamus is dating his 7,000-year span from the inception of Man, or from the birth of Christ. Either way, the world is moving inexorably towards its end, and the sum total of our human achievements will be neither significant, nor remembered, in its aftermath.

SUMMARY

The joke is on us. Everything humanity thought would last will be lost in the mists of time. We are simply part of a whole, and relevant, even to ourselves, no longer.

As soone as we to be begunne,

we did beginne to be undone.

ANON

INDEX

Page numbers in **bold** indicate
main entries

Abortion debate **76–8**
Abraham 61, 231
Adam 61, 179
Adams, Samuel 114
Aegean Sea 91, 131, 288, 336
Aesop's fables 139
Afghanistan 23, 25
Africa 66, 190
  birth of Pan-African leader **169–70**
Agamemnon 118
Al Serat 105
alchemy 3, 75, 126, 130, 176, 213, 270,
  272, 300, 345
Alexander of Hales 14
Alexander the Great 211, 242
Ali (Al Haòdara) 120
Ali Pasha 120
Alp Abslan 120
American War of Independence 270
Ammianus 84
Anglican Church (Church of England)
  43–4, 109
Anjou, Duke of 16
Annals of the Three Kingdoms (Il Jon) 56
Antichrist *see* third Antichrist
Aphrodite 88, 89, 179
Apollo 130, 200, 287, 324
Arab war **234–5**
Arethusa 19
Aristotle 77, 314
Ark of the Covenant 75
Armageddon 340–1, **344–5**
Artemis 61
Ascapart 113
assassination of a world leader **48–51**
asteroid strikes the Earth **256–7**
Australia 29, 111
  war with Indonesia 157–8
Aventinus (Johann Turmair) 93
Avertin, St 93
Aymes de Chavigny, Jean 13

Ba'athists 23, 27
Babylon 10, 211, 304
Bacchus 213

battle of the sexes **199–200**
Bellona 255
Benedict XVI (Joseph Ratzinger) **45–7**,
  54, 70, 80
  dangers to **67–8**
Bevis of Southampton, Sir **112–14**
Bhutto, Benazir 1, 50–51
Bhutto, Murtaza 50
Bhutto, Shahnawaz 50
Bible 38, 77, 202, 324
birth of an island **106–7**
book burning **201–2**
Brewer, E. Cobham 304
Britain/United Kingdom 25, 29, 31, 49,
  50, 113–14, 262, 306
  end of monarchy 5, **163–8**
  fails to exit the European Union **102–3**
  Fortress Britain 213, 268, **276–7**
  Franco-British crisis **331–2**
  succession to the throne **108–9**
Buddhism 77
  and the Protestant Church **226–7**
Burma's military junta **32–3**
Bush, George W. 1, 23, 29, 49, 50
Bush, Jeb, Governor of Florida 49, 50
Byron, Lord 88

Calvinism 227
Camoëns 38, 213
Canada 111, 316
Cancer 118
Cappel, Jacques 101
Casaubon, Isaac 14–15
Castor and Pollux 310
Catesby, Robert 166
Catherine de Medici 13, 16
Catholic/Roman Catholic Church 39, 46,
  47, 70, 80
  abortion debate reignites **76–8**
  aftermath of schism **100–1**
  Catholic/Jewish miscegenation **178–80**
  crisis 4–5, **216–25**
  healing of confederacy **102–3**
  scandals 90–5
Catholicism/Roman Catholicism 9, 10,
  11, 231
Centuries 3, 4, 13
change of world order **280–1**

Charlemagne 176
Charles, Prince (Charles III of England)
    72, 109
    abdication 110-1
Charles V of Germany 324
Charles VIII of France 10
Charles IX of France 16
Charlie Hebdo attack 99
Charon 123, 124
chemical warfare **175-7**, 179
China 149, 153, 174, 211, 215, 259
    and United States
        false dawn **208-9**
        see eye to eye 307-8
        standoff **206-7**
Christianity/Christians 19, 31, 38, 120,
    176, 213, 235, 322
Church of England *see* Anglican Church
Churchill, Winston 29
Cicero 56
civil disobedience begins **278-9**
class war 142-3
climate change 294, 296
    due to global war **282-3**
Clinton, Hillary Rodham **83-4**
Clytemnestra 118, 310
Coliseum, Rome 285, 287-8
collective unconscious **181-2**
College of Cardinals 70, 225
comets 174, 182
    41P/Tuttle-Giacobini-Kresak 53
Congress of Vienna 261-2
Constantine II of Greece 306
Constantino of Greece 306
Corpus Hermeticus 14-15
crescent moon 123, 215
Croatia 139
    Serbo-Croatian conflict **230-1**
Cyprus 160
    partition **305-6**
Czech Republic 292

Da Vinci, Leonardo 326
Daedalus 131
Dalmatia 139, 231
Demetrius 73
Diana, goddess 53-4, 61, 73, 118
Diana, Princess of Wales **71-3**, 111
Donne, John 340
Dryden, John 176

earthquakes 294, 296
    Europe 291-2
    US **295-6**
eclipses *see* solar eclipses
ecological disasters **85-9**, **317-8**
Egypt 149, 287
Egypt, ancient 10, 56, 233
Eliot, T. S. 343
Elizabeth II 109, 111
embryo replacement, dangers of **245-7**
Endymion 246
England
    secession from European Union 228-9,
        244, 332
    consequences **241-2**
    fall out with Scotland **248-9**
EURATOM 253
European earthquake **291-2**
European Union (EU) 50, 160, 231
England secedes **228-9**, 244, 332
    consequences **241-2**
    England and Scotland fall out **248-9**
    nuclear market 252-3
Evvoia (Euboea) 336

famine 66, 49, 242, 270
    great 213, **250-1**
    Mediterranean **335-6**
    famine relief **81-2**
Fawkes, Guy 166
Fayed, Dodi **71-3**
Fenris 340
Fescennine Verses 89
financial meltdown/credit crunch 2,
    58-9
First Family *see* new First Family
Fortress Britain *see* Britain
France 8-10, 49, 50, 61, 143, 145, 147,
    168, 213, 229, 237, 249, 251, 253, 336
    crisis 4, 318, **325-30**, **332-4**
    prelude **301-5**, **315-16**
    Franco-British crisis **331-2**
    immigration **193-4**
    leadership **232-4**
    political correctness **144-7**
    terrorist attack in southern **104-5**
    winter freeze **150-1**
Francis (pope) 39, 68, 80
Franco, General 143

Gabriel 215
Gautama Buddha 61, 227
Gemelle, Anne Ponsarde 12
Genesis 120, 179, 217, 304
Geneva Doctrines (1541) 227
Genoa 336
Germany 143, 176, 262
Global War 4, 153, 211, 240, **258–68**
  aftermath **269–70**
  and climate change **282–3**
  twenty years after **313–14**
  warnings **254–5**
global warming **61–2**, **189–92**, 312,
  335–6
Gnosticism 10–11
Gossaert, Jan (Mabuse) 237
great famine 213, **250–1**
great storm **161–2**
Greece
  Cyprus partition **305–6**
  Greco-Turkish problem **159–60**
  nuclear accident **311–12**
Greece/Greeks, ancient 10, 61, 126, 128,
  168, 270, 312, 314
Grégoire, Abbé Henri 9
Guantanamo Bay 22–3
Gunpowder Plot 166

Hades 123, 124, 272
Hamza 120–1
Henri de Navarre 16
Hercules 118
hermaphrodites 179
Hermes see Mercury
Hermes Trismegistus 274
Hero and Leander 88, 89
Hierocles 88
Hindus 174, 340
Hitler, Adolf 29, 64, 137, 143, 153,
  202, 203
Hungary in crisis **309–10**
Hussein, Saddam 23, 27, 29,
  31, 237

Ibn Hazm 46
Icarus 131
Indonesia 36, 107
  war with Australia **157–8**
Inquisition 4, 9, 10, 14
Interview, The 57
Iphigenia 118

Iran 149, 172, 227
Iraq 172, 235, 266
  US/Iraq War 23, **24–31**
Iris 89, 90, 176, 177
Isaac 231
Ishmael 231
Islam/Muslims 19, 21, 25, 46–7, 123, 139,
  172, 202, 205, 259, 304, 322
  disturbs balance of world power **210–15**
  emancipation of women **197–8**
  see also Shiites; Sunnis
Israel 50, 77, 180, 324
  future of **303–4**
Italy 149, 168, 285, 304, 338

James I 166
Jason of the Argonauts 88
Jerome, St 77
Jesus Christ 38, 61, 156, 223, 261, 322
Jews see Judaism
Joan of Arc (Jeanne la Pucelle) 164, 316,
  326, 331
John Paul I 68
John Paul II (Karol Wojtyla)
  aftermath of death **52–4**
  death **37–9**
John the Evangelist, St 64
Jovianus Pontanus 56
Judaism/Jews 9–10, 77, 194, 215, 322
  Catholic/Jewish miscegenation **178–80**
Judas Iscariot 302, 326
Jung, C. G. 182
Juno 118
Jupiter 89, 207, 213, 296

ḳabbalah 10–11
Katrina, hurricane 41
Khoury, Adel Theodore 46
Koran 46, 61, 172, 215
Kronos 66, 207

Lane, Libby 44
Lares 229
Last Supper, The (Da Vinci) 326
Libra 207
Ligurian arts 302
locust plagues 190, **293–4**, 296
Louis XII 10
Lunedi, St 61

Mab, Queen 237

Mabus, Raymond 237–8
Macron, Emmanuel **100–101**
Mafia killing **185–8**
Magi 39, 156
magic 14–16
Malachy, Saint 300
Manuel II Palaiologos 46
Marianne 316
Mars 39, 116, 118, 120, 213, 255
Marsili, Mount 285
Martha, St 38–9
McGregor, Robert (Rob Roy) 249
Mediterranean 105, 294
  famine **335–6**
Medusa 300
Mercury (Hermes) 72, 126, 130, 179, 213,
  272
Mesopotamia 235, 266
meteor strikes 174, 182
  as harbingers of change **183–4**
Midas, King of Phrygia 72
Middle East 149, 266, 273, 304, **323–4**
Mississippi floods 41
Mithraism 7
Mithridates 255
monsoon rains **204–5**
moon 123, 215, 340
Moses 61, 261
Mouterizes 46–7
Muhammad (Mohammed) 46, 61, 120,
  172, 215, 261
Muslims *see* Islam

Napoleon 60, 202, 261, 283
Neptune 207, 296
Nero 202
new First Family **117–8**
  precursor **115–16**
new leader appears **289–90**
New Orleans floods **40–41**
Nietzsche 182
nirvana 227
Noah 61
North Korean crisis 1–2, **55–7**
Nostradamus
  biographical notes 8–16
  leave-taking **339–41**
nuclear fission **74–5**
nuclear market in new Europe 245–6

Olympus (Olimbos), Mount 89

Orestes 118
Orion 53–4
Othman, Sultan 123
Ottoman Empire 123, 153, 259
'Owl and the Pussy-Cat, The' (Lear) 246

Pannonia 84
Paracelsus 126, 270
Paradise Lost (Milton) 130, 272
Paris 8, 72, 99, 213, 302
Parker Bowles, Camilla 109
Paul, Apostle 73
Paul, Crown Prince of Greece 306
peace reigns over the earth **239–40**
Pétain, Maréchal 143, 147
Philip, King of Macedon 281
philosopher's stone 133
  discovery of **125–6**
  secret lost **132–3**
Phocensian Despair 281
Phocis 99
Phoebus 209, 324
Phoenix Periods 270
plague 12, 105, 184, 251
Pliny the Elder (Publius Caecilius
  Secundus) 31, 36, 246
Pliny the Younger 36
Pluto 207, 227
political correctness **134–5**, **144–7**
Pope 217, 219, 221, 223, 225
  death of (2012) **69–70**, **79–80**
  final **299–300**
  see also Benedict XVI; John Paul II
Protestant Church
  Buddhism and **226–7**
  crisis 1–2, **42–4**
Ptolemies 304, 306
Ptolemy (Claudius Ptolemaeus) 97
Pythagoras 14, 38, 202, 227, 312

Ravenna 139
'red man' 283, 308
Red Sea 304
religious revival **60–62**
religious sect, emergence of new **321–2**
religious wars **171–4**
René, King 9, 10
Revelation of St John 86, 275
Rhodes 160, 287, 288, 336
Robinson, Gene 43, 44
Rome 38, 219, 285

Rome/Romans, ancient 168, 196, 202,
 233, 306, 310, 314
Russia 31, 84, 143, 174, 176, 262, 320

Safa, Mount 261
Sagittarius 86
Saint-Rémy, Jean de 10
Saqer, Sheik Abu 47
Satan 120, 174
 the great comedian **342–3**
Saturn 56, 66, 207
Schori, Katherine Jefferts 44
Scotland 229
 fall out with England over European
  Union **248–9**
Scott, Walter 172
secularization of superstate **319–20**
Selene (Luna) 123, 246
Serbia 139
 Serbo-Croatian conflict **230–1**
Shakespeare 113, 172, 188, 326
Sharia 172
Shiites 172, 231
 Sunni/Shiite war **119–20**
six lucky gamblers **122–4**
solar eclipses 93, 149, 158, 170
Spain 143, 168, 338
Spencer, Lord 72
St Elmo's Fire 156, 310
Stalin 64, 143, 202, 320
submarine warfare **337–8**
Suez Canal 66
sun 120, **127–31**, 340
 blotted out **132–3**
Sun Kyi, Aung San **32–4**
Sunnis 172
 Sunni/Shiite war **119–20**
Surabaya 158
Surtsey 107
Syria 235, 266

Taliban 23, 198
Talmud 179
Tangun Wanggom 56
Tarascon 38
terrorism **195–6**, 198
 southern France attack **104–5**
third Antichrist 202–3, 264, 266, **271–5**,
 302, 324
 advance warning **63–4**
 aftermath of the coming **297–8**

birth **152–4**
consequences **155–6**
presages **136–9**, 148–9
Thomas, St 77
Traité des Fardemens (Nostradamus) 13
Trasimeno, Lake 186
Treaties of Rome
 (1957) 244, 246
 (2065) **243–4**
Trump, Donald 84, 89, 91
tsunamis **35–6**, **284–8**
Turkey 123, 235, 266, 288
 Cyprus partition 305–6
 Greco-Turkish problem **159–60**
Tuttle, Horace 53
Twin Towers disaster 2, **18–21**

United Kingdom *see* Britain
United Nations 231, 338
United States 114, 153, 168, 174, 211,
 215, 249, 259
 and China
  false dawn **208–9**
  see eye to eye **307–8**
  standoff **206–7**
 earthquake **295–6**
 hurricanes **191–2**
 Iraq War 23, **24–31**
 presidential election (2032) **140–1**

Velleius Paterculus 84
Venus 66, 120, 126, 168, 200
Vesuvius 36
Vulcan 118, 130

Wall Street crash 59, 296
William, Prince (William V of England)
 111, 164
winter freeze **150–1**
world order *see* change of world order
World War Two 143, 147, 268
worldwide epidemic **236–8**

Zardari, Asif Ali 51

WATKINS
Sharing Wisdom Since 1893

The story of Watkins began in 1893, when scholar of esotericism John Watkins founded our bookshop, inspired by the lament of his friend and teacher Madame Blavatsky that there was nowhere in London to buy books on mysticism, occultism or metaphysics. That moment marked the birth of Watkins, soon to become the publisher of many of the leading lights of spiritual literature, including Carl Jung, Rudolf Steiner, Alice Bailey and Chögyam Trungpa.

Today, the passion at Watkins Publishing for vigorous questioning is still resolute. Our stimulating and groundbreaking list ranges from ancient traditions and complementary medicine to the latest ideas about personal development, holistic wellbeing and consciousness exploration. We remain at the cutting edge, committed to publishing books that change lives.

DISCOVER MORE AT:
www.watkinspublishing.com

| Read our blog | Watch and listen to our authors in action | Sign up to our mailing list |

We celebrate conscious, passionate, wise and happy living.
Be part of that community by visiting

 /watkinspublishing   @watkinswisdom

 /watkinsbooks   @watkinswisdom